50 WALKS IN
Sussex &
the South Downs

50 Walks in Sussex & the South Downs

Published by AA Publishing (a trading name of AA Media Limited, whose registered office is Grove House, Lutyens Close, Lychpit, Basingstoke, Hampshire RG24 8AG; registered number 06112600)

© AA Media Limited 2019
First published 2001
Second edition 2008
Third edition 2013
This edition 2019, reprinted 2021

Field checked and updated by Dixe Wills

Mapping in this book is derived from the following products:
OS Landranger 186 (walks 32, 38, 42, 47)
OS Landranger 187 (walks 19, 25)
OS Landranger 188 (walk 18)
OS Landranger 189 (walks 1-2)
OS Landranger 197 (walks 33, 35-37, 39-41, 43-46, 48-50)
OS Landranger 198 (walks 16-17, 20-24, 26-31, 34)
OS Landranger 199 (walks 3-9, 11–15)
OS Explorer 8 (walk 46)
OS Explorer 25 (walk 10)

© Crown copyright and database rights 2019 Ordnance Survey. 100021153.

ISBN: 978-0-7495-8124-4
ISBN (SS): 978-0-7495-7513-7

Series management: Donna Wood
Editor: Liz Jones
Designer: Tom Whitlock
Digital imaging & repro: Ian Little
Cartography provided by the Mapping Services Department of AA Publishing

Printed and bound in the UK by Bell & Bain Ltd, Glasgow

A05792

We would like to thank the following photographers, companies and picture libraries for their assistance in the preparation of this book. Abbreviations for the picture credits are as follows:
Alamy = Alamy Stock Photo
12/13 Liliya Sayfeeva/Alamy; 29 Chris Dorney/Alamy; 45 Joana Kruse/Alamy; 61 Dave Porter/Alamy; 71 Tony Watson/Alamy; 91 Glenn Driver/Alamy; 101 imageBROKER/Alamy; 111 Peter Marjoram/Alamy; 121 Genevieve Vallee/Alamy; 131 chris gorman/Alamy; 147 Dave Porter/Alamy; 162 picture that/Alamy

The contents of this book are believed correct at the time of printing. Nevertheless, the publishers cannot be held responsible for any errors or omissions or for changes in the details given in this book or for the consequences of any reliance on the information it provides. This does not affect your statutory rights. We have tried to ensure accuracy in this book, but things do change and we would be grateful if readers would advise us of any inaccuracies they may encounter by emailing walks@aamediagroup.co.uk

We have done our best to make sure that these walks are safe and achievable by walkers with a basic level of fitness. However, we can accept no responsibility for any loss or injury incurred while following the walks. Advice on walking safely can be found on pages 10–11.

Some of the walks may appear in other AA books and publications.

Discover and book AA-rated places to stay at RatedTrips.com

AA

50 WALKS IN
Sussex & the
South Downs

CONTENTS

How to use this book   6

Exploring the area   8

Walking in safety   10

The walks

WALK		GRADIENT	DISTANCE	PAGE
1	Rye Harbour	Negligible	4.5 miles (7.2km)	14
2	Winchelsea	▲	4.5 miles (7.2km)	17
3	Hastings	▲▲	4 miles (6.4km)	20
4	Great Dixter	▲	3 miles (4.8km)	23
5	Battle	▲	5 miles (8km)	26
6	Burwash	▲▲	4.75 miles (7.7km)	30
7	Brightling	▲	5 miles (8km)	33
8	Herstmonceux	▲	3 miles (4.8km)	36
9	Pevensey	Negligible	4.5 miles (7.2km)	39
10	Birling Gap	▲▲	7 miles (11.2km)	42
11	Jevington	▲▲	3 miles (4.8km)	46
12	Wilmington	▲▲	6.25 miles (10km)	49
13	Arlington	▲	3 miles (4.8km)	52
14	Alfriston and Berwick	▲▲	4 miles (6.4km)	55
15	Cuckmere Haven	▲▲	5.25 miles (8.5km)	58
16	Firle Tower	▲▲	4.75 miles (7.6km)	62
17	Firle Downlands	▲▲	3.75 miles (6km)	65
18	Ashdown Forest	▲	7 miles (11.3km)	68
19	Forest Row	▲	5.5 miles (8.8km)	72
20	Barcombe Mills	Negligible	2.75 miles (4.4km)	75
21	Blackcap	▲▲▲	8.5 miles (13.7km)	78
22	Rodmell	▲	3 miles (4.8km)	81

WALK		GRADIENT	DISTANCE	PAGE
23	Around Rottingdean	▲	5 miles (8km)	84
24	Ditchling	▲▲	5 miles (8km)	87
25	Horsted Keynes	▲	5 miles (8km)	92
26	Cuckfield	▲▲	5 miles (8km)	95
27	Brighton	▲	3 miles (4.8km)	98
28	Devil's Dyke	▲▲▲	2.75 miles (4.4km)	102
29	Bramber	Negligible	2.5 miles (4km)	105
30	Cissbury Ring	▲▲	8.5 miles (13.7km)	108
31	Shipley	▲	7 miles (11.3km)	112
32	Loxwood	▲	4.5 miles (7.2km)	115
33	Parham	▲▲	5.5 miles (8.8km)	118
34	Highdown Hill	▲	2.25 miles (3.6km)	122
35	Climping	Negligible	4 miles (6.4km)	125
36	Arundel	▲▲	5.5 miles (8.9km)	128
37	Amberley	▲▲▲	6.5 miles (10.5km)	132
38	Ebernoe Common	▲	3.5 miles (5.7km)	135
39	Petworth	▲	3.5 miles (5.7km)	138
40	Bignor	▲▲	5.25 miles (8.5km)	141
41	Slindon	▲▲	5.5 miles (8.9km)	144
42	Black Down	▲▲	6 miles (9.7km)	148
43	Midhurst	▲	3 miles (4.8km)	151
44	Goodwood	▲	5 miles (8km)	154
45	East Lavant	▲	5 miles (8km)	157
46	Chichester	Negligible	4 miles (6.4km)	160
47	Shulbrede Priory	▲▲	2.75 miles (4.4km)	164
48	Kingley Vale	▲▲	5 miles (8km)	167
49	West Itchenor	Negligible	3.5 miles (5.7km)	170
50	West Wittering	Negligible	5 miles (8km)	173

HOW TO USE THIS BOOK

Each walk starts with an information panel giving all the information you will need about the walk at a glance, including its relative difficulty, distance and total amount of ascent. Difficulty levels and gradients are as follows:

Difficulty of walk

● Easy

◐ Intermediate

● Hard

Gradient

▲ Some slopes

▲▲ Some steep slopes

▲▲▲ Several very steep slopes

Maps

Every walk has its own route map. We also suggest a relevant AA or Ordnance Survey map to take with you, allowing you to view the area in more detail. The time suggested is the minimum for reasonably fit walkers and doesn't allow for stops.

Route map legend

- - →- -	Walk route	▨	Built-up area
❶	Route waypoint	▨	Woodland area
- - - -	Adjoining path	👥	Toilet
•	Place of interest	🅿	Car park
⌂	Steep section	⊞	Picnic area
⧭	Viewpoint	)(	Bridge

Start points

The start of each walk is given as a six-figure grid reference prefixed by two letters referring to a 100km square of the National Grid. More information on grid references can be found on most OS and AA Walker's Maps.

Dogs

We have tried to give dog owners useful advice about how dog friendly each walk is. Please respect other countryside users. Keep your dog under control, especially around livestock, and obey local bylaws and other dog control notices.

Car parking

Many of the car parks suggested are public, but occasionally you may have to park on the roadside or in a lay-by. Please be considerate about where you leave your car, ensuring that you are not on private property or access roads, and that gates are not blocked and other vehicles can pass safely.

Walks locator map

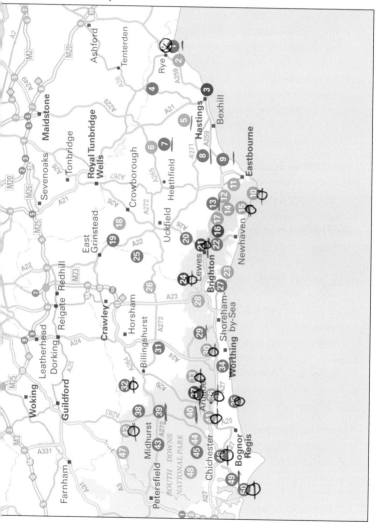

EXPLORING THE AREA

Divided into East and West Sussex back in 1888 for administrative purposes, Sussex is so typically English that to walk through its landscape will feel like a walk through the whole country. Within its boundaries lies a wide variety of landscape and coastal scenery, but it is the spacious and open South Downs with which Sussex is most closely associated.

This swathe of breezy downland represents some of the finest walking in southern England – an oasis of green in the midst of encroaching urban development. Designated an Area of Outstanding Natural Beauty and awarded full National Park status in 2011, the 90-mile (144km) chain of the Downs provides locals, as well as the many visitors, with a perfect natural playground. Kite flyers, model-aircraft enthusiasts, cyclists and hang-gliders are among the crowds who flock to these windswept chalk uplands.

Inspirational Sussex

It is walkers who are probably most at home here. Wooded in the west and bare and exposed in the east, the Downs offer miles of exhilarating walking. A bracing hike along the ridge of these hills is often accompanied by the faint tang of the sea and magnificent views of the coast and the Weald. The writer Hilaire Belloc regarded the South Downs as a national institution, which lifted people's experience and understanding of them to something approaching a religious creed. He wrote of Sussex as if it were the 'crown of England'.

Another writer whose love affair with Sussex lasted a lifetime was Rudyard Kipling. Perhaps the best way to see his 'blunt, bow-headed, whale-backed Downs' is from the South Downs Way, which runs like a thread across the ridge of the hills and is one of Britain's most popular long-distance trails. However, the South Downs can be seen and admired from countless vantage points, and for anyone who loves and appreciates the English landscape, a glimpse of a dramatic downland escarpment against the sky leaves a lasting impression.

Sussex landscapes

While some of the best walking will be found on the South Downs, there are many opportunities to explore the rest of Sussex on foot. The walks in this guide reach every corner of the county, from the gentle coastal terrain of Chichester Harbour to the glorious wooded landscape of Ashdown Forest.

The routes are designed to capture the essence and spirit of Sussex, visiting many of its famous landmarks and revealing the diversity of its splendid scenery. Every aspect of its history and geology is recorded. All that has shaped and influenced this county over the centuries is here.

Specific themes

It may be something of a cliché, but walking remains our most popular outdoor activity. There is little to add to this statistic, save to say that one of its greatest pleasures is the opportunity to learn so much more about the countryside. A really good walk should be educational, enjoyable and informative, providing a unique insight into the changing character of our rural landscape.

Each route in this book offers a specific theme to enhance the walk, as well as lots of snippets of useful information on what to look for and what to do while you're there. All the walks are circular and almost all are rural rambles, but if you prefer a city stroll, there are town walks in historic Chichester and vibrant Brighton to enjoy. Above all, take your time and savour the many delights that Sussex offers the explorer on foot.

Waymarking signs

On your walks around Sussex, you will see various waymarking signs. Blue arrows indicate bridleways, which are suitable for walkers, cyclists and horse-riders; yellow arrows indicate footpaths, suitable for walkers only; red arrows indicate byways, open to all traffic; and acorn markers indicate national trails, such as the South Downs Way.

PUBLIC TRANSPORT

Sussex is well served by public transport, making many of the walks in this guide easily accessible. The Winchelsea, Hastings, Battle, Pevensey, Arlington, Lewes (Blackcap), Horsted Keynes, Brighton, Arundel, Amberley and Chichester walks (routes 2, 3, 5, 9, 13, 21, 25, 27, 36, 37 and 46) start at a railway station or near to one.

For times of trains throughout Sussex visit nationalrail.co.uk or southernrailway.com. For bus times visit traveline.info.

WALKING IN SAFETY

All these walks are suitable for any reasonably fit person, but less experienced walkers should try the easier walks first. Route-finding is usually straightforward, but you will find that an Ordnance Survey or AA walking map is a useful addition to the route maps and descriptions; recommendations can be found in the information panels.

Risks

Although each walk here has been researched with a view to minimising the risks to the walkers who follow its route, no walk in the countryside can be considered to be completely free from risk. Walking in the outdoors will always require a degree of common sense and judgement to ensure that it is as safe as possible.

- Be particularly careful on cliff paths and in upland terrain, where the consequences of a slip can be very serious.

- Remember to check tidal conditions before walking on the seashore.

- Some sections of route are by, or cross, busy roads. Take care, and remember that traffic is a danger even on minor country lanes.

- Be careful around farmyard machinery and livestock, especially if you have children with you.

- Be aware of the consequences of changes in the weather, and check the forecast before you set out. Carry spare clothing and a torch if you are walking in the winter months. Remember that the weather can change very quickly at any time of the year, and in moorland and heathland areas, mist and fog can make route-finding much harder. Don't set out in these conditions unless you are confident of your navigation skills in poor visibility.

- In summer remember to take account of the heat and sun; wear a hat and carry water.

- On walks away from centres of population you should carry a whistle and survival bag. If you do have an accident that means you require help from the emergency services, make a note of your position as accurately as possible and dial 999.

Countryside Code
Respect other people:

- Consider the local community and other people enjoying the outdoors.

- Co-operate with people at work in the countryside. For example, keep out of the way when farm animals are being gathered or moved, and follow directions from the farmer.

- Don't block gateways, driveways or other paths with your vehicle.
- Leave gates and property as you find them, and follow paths unless wider access is available, such as on open country or registered common land (known as 'open access land').
- Leave machinery and farm animals alone – don't interfere with animals, even if you think they're in distress. Try to alert the farmer instead.
- Use gates, stiles or gaps in field boundaries if you can – climbing over walls, hedges and fences can damage them and increase the risk of farm animals escaping.
- Our heritage matters to all of us – be careful not to disturb ruins and historic sites.

Protect the natural environment:
- Take your litter home. Litter and leftover food don't just spoil the beauty of the countryside; they can be dangerous to wildlife and farm animals. Dropping litter and dumping rubbish are criminal offences.
- Leave no trace of your visit, and take special care not to damage, destroy or remove features such as rocks, plants and trees.
- Keep dogs under effective control, making sure they are not a danger or nuisance to farm animals, horses, wildlife or other people.
- If cattle or horses chase you and your dog, it is safer to let your dog off the lead – don't risk getting hurt by trying to protect it. Your dog will be much safer if you let it run away from a farm animal in these circumstances, and so will you.
- Everyone knows how unpleasant dog mess is and it can cause infections, so always clean up after your dog and get rid of the mess responsibly – bag it and bin it.
- Fires can be as devastating to wildlife and habitats as they are to people and property – so be careful with naked flames and cigarettes at any time of the year.

Enjoy the outdoors:
- Plan ahead and be prepared for natural hazards, changes in weather and other events.
- Wild animals, farm animals and horses can behave unpredictably if you get too close, especially if they're with their young – so give them plenty of space.
- Follow advice and local signs.

For more information visit naturalengland.org.uk/ourwork/enjoying/countrysidecode

LAGOONS AT RYE HARBOUR

DISTANCE/TIME	4.5 miles (7.2km) / 2hrs
ASCENT/GRADIENT	Negligible
PATHS	Level paths and good, clear tracks
LANDSCAPE	Mixture of shingle expanses and old gravel workings, now part of a local nature reserve
SUGGESTED MAP	OS Explorer 125 Romney Marsh, Rye & Winchelsea
START/FINISH	Grid reference: TQ942189
DOG FRIENDLINESS	Dogs on lead within Rye Harbour Nature Reserve
PARKING	Spacious free car park at Rye Harbour
PUBLIC TOILETS	Rye Harbour – turn left out of the car park

Turn the clock back to the dark days of World War II, and you would find Rye Harbour a very different place. Blockhouses for machine guns littered the coast, and barbed wire and landmines made it a 'no go' area. During the hours of darkness, great searchlights swept across the night sky; they were particularly effective at detecting the dreaded flying bombs. Go there now and you can still identify some of these crumbling relics of war. It's a fascinating exercise to rewrite the pages of history and imagine what might have happened if enemy forces had landed on this forgotten corner of England.

World War II wasn't the first time the area had been under threat. During the Napoleonic Wars, 150 years earlier, Rye Harbour was considered a target for invasion and attack when the Martello tower, seen by the car park at the start of the walk, became the first of 47 fortifications built in Sussex as a defence against the French. The tower would certainly have been a tough deterrent. The walls are nearly 12ft (4m) thick at the base, and the middle floor would have been occupied by a garrison of one officer and 24 men. Since then, the sea has built up over half a mile (800m) of land in front of it, with violent storms dumping huge deposits of shingle on the shore every winter.

Today, the little community of Rye Harbour is peaceful – and yet, many decades after the end of the war, it still conveys that same sense of bleak isolation. Though not as atmospheric as neighbouring shingle-strewn Dungeness, it does feel very isolated here. Part of a designated Site of Special Scientific Interest (SSSI), Rye Harbour Nature Reserve lies at the mouth of the River Rother, which forms its eastern boundary. During its early stage, the walk follows the river, and at first glance the shingle seems so bare and inhospitable that it is hard to imagine any plant could grow here. But in late May and June the beach is transformed by a colourful array of flowers. Delicate yellow horned poppies, sea kale, carpets of seaweed and countless other species of plants thrive in this habitat. Salt marsh, vegetation along the river's edge, pools and grazing marsh add to the variety, and the old gravel pits now represent an important site for nesting terns, gulls, ducks and waders. Rye Harbour is best known for its superb bird life, and is always very popular with ornithologists. The walk follows the coast for some time, passing the Ternery Pool, originally two separate gravel workings dug by hand early in the 20th century. It continues along the coast before heading inland to some more flooded gravel pits. Here you might easily spot gulls, grebes, cormorants, swallows and reed warblers. Turtle doves are often seen in the fields, and sometimes perch in pairs on the overhead wires.

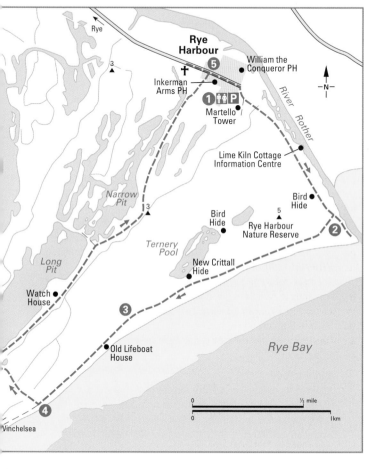

1. Keeping the Martello Tower and the entrance to the holiday village on your right, enter Rye Harbour Local Nature Reserve. The Rother can be seen on the left, running parallel to the path, with a wind farm visible behind. Head for the Rye Harbour Nature Reserve information centre and continue on the firm path, with the Rother still visible on the left. The expanse of Camber Sands, a popular holiday destination, nudges into view beyond the river mouth.

2. Near the river mouth, the route continues to the right along a private road marked with a 20mph sign, but first make a detour to the beach. Return to the

junction and follow the private road, which has permissive access for walkers, and cuts between wildlife sanctuary areas where access is not allowed. Pass the entrance to the New Crittall hide on the right. From here there are superb views over Ternery Pool, and Rye's jumble of houses can be seen sprawling over the hill in the distance. Continue west on the private road, which gradually edges nearer the shore.

3. Ahead now is the outline of the old abandoned lifeboat house and, away to the right in the distance, the unmistakable profile of Camber Castle. Keep going on the road.

4. Just after the fence on the right ends, take the waymarked footpath on the right (by a map information board, running towards a line of houses on the eastern side of the village of Winchelsea Beach) and head inland, passing a small pond on the right. Glancing back, the old lifeboat house can be seen standing out starkly against the sky. Turn right at the next junction along power lines, pass the Watch House and continue on the track as it runs alongside several lakes. Pass to the left of some dilapidated farm outbuildings and keep going along the track. Where the track forks, keep left on the main track, now leaving the power lines. The lakes are still seen on the left-hand side. Begin the approach to Rye Harbour; on the left is the spire of the church.

5. On reaching the road in the centre of the village of Rye Harbour, turn left to visit the lifeboatmen's memorial in the churchyard before heading back along the main street. Pass the Inkerman Arms and return to the car park at the start of the walk.

Where to eat and drink

The Inkerman Arms at Rye Harbour specialises in locally caught fresh fish. Food is available both at lunchtime and in the evening. Also in Rye Harbour, the William the Conqueror pub serves food, and the nearby Bosun's Bite café offers snacks and all-day breakfasts. The Gallery & Tea Room near the car park serves light refreshments from Thursday to Sunday.

What to see

Summer visitors to Rye Harbour include three types of tern, and there are other ground-nesting birds such as ringed plover, oystercatcher, redshank, avocet and lapwing. This is a good place to observe migration, and in winter large numbers of wildfowl and waders gather.

While you're there

Stop and look at the old lifeboat station beside the route of the walk. It's not been used since one stormy night in November 1928 when the 17-strong crew of the Mary Stanford were called to rescue a leaking steamer. The volunteers dragged the lifeboat into the sea through gale force winds and huge waves. Soon afterwards, the coastguard heard the steamer was safe, but with no ship-to-shore radio he was unable to tell the lifeboat crew. The next day, the Mary Stanford was seen floating upside down. Not one volunteer survived the tragedy.

WINCHELSEA'S LAND-LOCKED PORT

DISTANCE/TIME	4.5 miles (7.2km) / 2hrs
ASCENT/GRADIENT	197ft (60m) / ▲
PATHS	Field paths and pavements, several stiles
LANDSCAPE	Mixture of marshland and undulating farmland
SUGGESTED MAPS	OS Explorer 124 Hastings & Bexhill
START/FINISH	Grid reference: TQ905173
DOG FRIENDLINESS	On lead near birding hide and across farmland
PARKING	Roadside parking near St Thomas's Church at Winchelsea
PUBLIC TOILETS	Winchelsea

The story of Winchelsea is fascinating: surely nowhere else in the country can have fallen victim to fate in quite the same way. Looking at the town today, it is hard to believe it was once a thriving port, one of the most important on the south coast. It is one of seven Cinque Ports, characterised by elegant houses and a grid of quiet streets, and became stranded when the sea receded, exposing a stretch of marshland. Now it lies more than a mile (1.6km) inland.

This new town had replaced Old Winchelsea in the late 13th century, when it was inundated by the sea in a great storm in 1287. The older town now lies beneath the English Channel, out in Rye Bay. As the water encroached, the inhabitants built new homes on the hilltop, establishing themselves on higher ground. The new town was conceived and sited personally by Edward I, and, with its regular grid pattern, has long been acknowledged as perhaps the first example of medieval English town planning. Only a dozen of the proposed 39 grid squares were ever completed, and the ambitious plans for the new Winchelsea were eventually abandoned. Three gates, part of the original fortification, still survive, including Strand Gate with its four round towers. Many of the buildings seen today date from the 17th and 18th centuries, but a number are built over earlier medieval wine cellars.

The town's bad luck continued through the Middle Ages, when Winchelsea came under constant attack from the French and suffered heavy damage. The church, much of which was destroyed during the last raid of 1449, includes the tomb of Gervase Alard, England's first admiral, as well as various monuments and a wall painting from the 14th century.

Before starting the walk, take a leisurely tour round the town – the views from Strand Gate out towards the Channel are very impressive. This is a walk of two extremes. From Winchelsea's lofty vantage point, you'll descend to a bare, rather featureless landscape, skirting a flat expanse of water-meadows known as Pett Level. The return leg is more undulating, with good views of both the coast and Winchelsea's unspoiled hilltop setting.

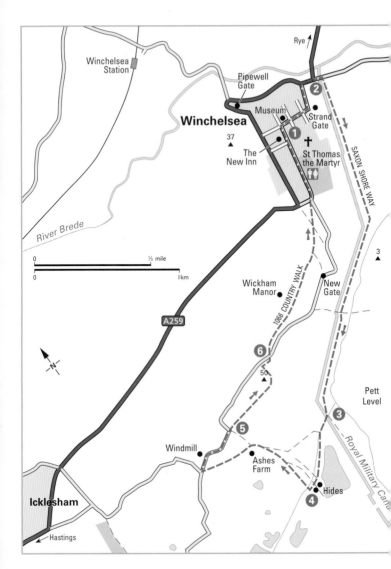

1. With The New Inn on your left, and St Thomas's Church on your right, follow the road round the right-hand bend. Head down to Strand Gate, then take the road to the junction with the A259. Turn right and follow the pavement along.

2. When the road bends left, turn right into a road signed 'Winchelsea Beach'. Just after crossing the Royal Military Canal, turn right. Follow the tow path across this empty landscape. At the first path junction, avoid the concrete footbridge. Eventually, the canal begins to curve left.

3. Just after the next pinch-gate, turn right over the footbridge, then take the left-hand footbridge and proceed alongside a water channel.

4. After two hides in quick succession on your left, cross a footbridge, keep right on the other side, then soon bear left and follow the path through the

reed beds. Begin a moderate climb and head towards a house. Keep to the left of it and follow the path through the trees. This veers right in front of some private gates and up some steps to a stile; turn left along the field-edge to a kissing gate. Cross a drive, go through a gate and bear half right across the field to a stile buried in a hedge in the top corner. Continue on an overgrown path between fences, crossing two further stiles. Bear right to skirt the field to the next stile and exit to the road through a barely discernible gap in the hedge. Keep right here, signposted 'Winchelsea', and pass below the hilltop windmill, soon joining the 1066 Country Walk that comes in from the left and continues along the road.

5. Go straight ahead over a stile when the lane bends left, cross the field to a stile and keep along the left edge of two fields. Continue ahead down the gentle field slope.

6. Exit onto a road and turn right along it for a few paces to a stile on the left. Bear right, still on the 1066 Country Walk, and cross the next stile. Keep to the right of Wickham Manor and look for a stile in the far boundary. Cross the drive to a stile and keep ahead across the field to a kissing gate and a five-bar gate in the bottom left corner, to the left of the medieval New Gate. Follow the 1066 Country Walk waymarks. The path veers left of this hummocky field, eventually crossing a pair of stiles up on the right. Bear left in Chapel Field and begin a moderate ascent to a stone and wood stile beside a large remnant of medieval wall that once belonged to an almshouse called St John's Hospital. Turn right at the road, follow it round to the left and return to the centre of Winchelsea.

Where to eat and drink

At the very start or end of the walk you can call in at The New Inn for home-cooked dishes, cakes, cream teas and ice cream. The pub also has a large beer garden.

What to see

The Royal Military Canal runs below Winchelsea and extends for 25 miles (40km). Constructed at the beginning of the 19th century, its purpose was to protect the exposed southeast coast from invasion by Napoleon's forces. William Cobbett mentions the canal in his *Rural Rides*, wondering how a 30ft (9m)-wide ditch could possibly deter troops who had managed to cross the Rhine and the Danube. The Saxon Shore Way follows the tow path.

While you're there

Visit the Winchelsea Court Hall Museum, which highlights over 700 years of the Cinque Port's history. Models, maps, pictures, artefacts and memorabilia illustrate the history of the town. Call into the bird hide, part of the Pannel Valley Reserve. From here, you will probably be able to spot teals, coots, shelducks or geese on the water.

3

HASTINGS OLD TOWN AND HILL

DISTANCE/TIME	4 miles (6.4km) / 2hrs 30min
ASCENT/GRADIENT	328ft (100m) / ▲ ▲
PATHS	Tracks, minor roads and coastal paths
LANDSCAPE	High ground overlooking coast, with glens revealing layers of sandstone
SUGGESTED MAP	OS Explorer 124 Hastings & Bexhill
START/FINISH	Grid reference: TQ829094
DOG FRIENDLINESS	Return walk, along coast path, is ideal for dogs off lead
PARKING	Pay-and-display car park at Roc-a-Nore Road, Hastings
PUBLIC TOILETS	In Hastings, by car park at start of walk

Hastings has a real smack of the sea, with seagulls wheeling around fishing boats drawn up on the beach, known as the Stade, and a hugely characterful Old Town. Occupying a valley just to the east of the main part of town, this is a fascinating maze of tiny alleys, lanes and stepped paths with tiny cottage gardens and buildings spanning several centuries. Look out, for example, for the tiny Piece of Cheese House at 10 Starr Cottages (just off All Saints Street), named for its resemblance to a wedge of cheese, both in shape and colour.

The town is familiar to many as the backdrop of the TV series *Foyle's War*. The western part of Hastings includes the predominantly Victorian resort town and the area of St Leonards, dominated by a huge apartment block erected in the 1930s. Known as Marine Court, it was designed to resemble an ocean liner. Hastings' two town museums are both free to enter: one is on the High Street in the Old Town, while the other occupies a larger building in the newer part of town and contains the sumptuously ornate Durbar Hall, erected for the Indian and Colonial Exhibition in 1886. The Stade itself is home to Europe's largest beach-launched fishing fleet, and makes for an enjoyable stroll, with its photogenic array of lobster pots, weather-beaten craft and fishing nets hanging out to dry. The net shops, which stand near the boats on the shingle beach, are not really shops at all but huts used for storing fishing nets and tackle. The huts, intentionally tall and narrow to reduce ground rent, are unique, being found only in Hastings. Two of them are often opened up for visitors to see; one of them, known as Half Sovereign Cottage, is formed of half a boat. Alongside them, the Jerwood Gallery houses a notable collection of modern British art in a sleek modern building clad with black ceramic tiles, designed to blend with the neighbouring net shops.

Hastings, most unusually, has the distinction of having two cliff railways. One ascends West Hill, reaching an expanse of lawn close to the ruins of Hastings Castle, part of which has crumbled over the cliff edge. On the East Hill is Britain's steepest cliff railway; the journey is simple, short and straightforward and the views are magnificent. It takes you up to the start of the walk (note – it does not operate on weekdays in winter), above which are the only sandstone cliffs in southeast England; they have quite a different look to anywhere else in the region. Hastings is fortunate to have such dramatic scenery close by.

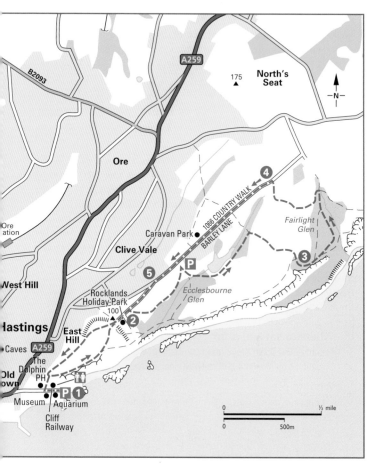

1. Turn left out of the car park, along Roc-a-Nore Road, to the East Hill cliff railway. Either take the ride to the top, or walk up. (If you prefer to walk, carry on along the road a few paces past the Dolphin Inn, then right up Tamarisk Steps, following the sign to East Hill half way up; at the top turn left on the road, then right up more steps to ascend to the upper cliff railway station.) Keep right up more steps, and follow the Fish Trail guideposts along the southern slopes of East Hill, with the sea on your right. Pass a beacon on your left and head steadily uphill.

2. Follow a diversion sign on which Ecclesbourne Glen and other places are mentioned. Pass the back entrance to Rocklands Holiday Park. Immediately afterwards turn right on an unmarked path that bears left. Keep going straight

ahead, following landslip diversion signs. At a fingerpost turn right through a kissing gate with a diversion sign on it. Immediately fork left. At a guidepost on a junction of paths, ignore the kissing gate to your left and turn right. Continue descending across a path, over a boardwalk and a confluence of paths to climb steadily to pass a pond. Turn sharp right uphill at a guidepost 9 towards Fairlight Glen. Leave the woods shortly afterwards to climb a wide grassy path with pasture to your left. Cross a footbridge and head on past guidepost 10 to go through a kissing gate and into woods. Descend to a junction at guidepost 12 and turn left. Drop down some steps and ignore the path to the left.

3. At the bottom of Fairlight Glen, turn left at bollard 16 just before a stream signposted 'Barley Lane', up the glen. Ignore some steps leading down to the right and, just after, turn sharp left at a junction by bollard 15 (ahead here is a map). Follow the track out of the woods, keeping forward at some gates.

4. Reach Barley Lane and turn left along it. Carry on past a caravan park and Barley Lane car park.

5. Just after passing a path on the right signposted 'Harold Road' (which you ignore), fork left into Rocklands Lane (with a 15mph speed limit sign). Soon you will gain a view over the sprawling jumble of rooftops, with rows of terraced houses scattered over the slopes and hillsides. This is residential Hastings. Pass to the right of the entrance of Rocklands Holiday Park and keep on the upper track at the fork. Cross the grassy expanse of East Hill by aiming slightly right. Much of the town can be seen down below, creating an impressive picture. Keep to the right of the beacon passed earlier and reach the top of the East Hill cliff railway, either travelling on it to return or taking the steps just to the right to zig-zag to the bottom.

Where to eat and drink
Hastings Old Town has a good choice, with the Lord Nelson and The Dolphin pubs near the cliff railway, and options on the High Street.

What to see
On East Hill above Hastings is a beacon, erected in 1988 to commemorate the 400th anniversary of the Spanish Armada. The original beacon was found at nearby North Seat. The hill also marks the site of an Iron Age settlement, established by Celts in about 40 B. Defended by earth banks and the cliff face, the site occupied a prominent position overlooking a natural harbour.

While you're there
Visit the Fishermen's Museum, which shows the history of fishing on this coast. In the Middle Ages, Hastings was an important harbour, and fishing is still a major industry here. The town has the largest beach-launched fishing fleet in Europe. Next to it are the Shipwreck Museum, with an array of objects found locally, and the Blue Reef aquarium, where you can walk through a glass tunnel beneath a spectacular 'reef pool'. Visit the caverns at the Smugglers Adventure in Hastings Old Town, and experience smuggling as it was over 200 years ago.

GREAT DIXTER'S GARDENS

DISTANCE/TIME	3 miles (4.8km) / 1hr 30min
ASCENT/GRADIENT	98ft (30m) / ▲
PATHS	Field paths and quiet roads
LANDSCAPE	Undulating farmland and stretches of woodland
SUGGESTED MAP	OS Explorer 125 Romney Marsh, Rye & Winchelsea
START/FINISH	Grid reference: TQ829245
DOG FRIENDLINESS	Dog stiles near Great Dixter and on Sussex Border Path
PARKING	Free car park on corner of Fullers Lane and A28, Northiam
PUBLIC TOILETS	Great Dixter, seasonal opening

Deep in the tranquil, rolling countryside of East Sussex, close to the Kent border, lies the wonderful Great Dixter, one of the county's smaller and more intimate historic houses. Built in the middle of the 15th century and later restored and enlarged by Sir Edwin Lutyens, Great Dixter is a popular tourist attraction as well as a family home.

These days this fine Wealden hall-house is owned and cared for by the Great Dixter Charitable Trust, which was set up by the late Christopher Lloyd, the gardening writer, who died in 2006. In 1910 Christopher's father, Nathaniel, had instructed Lutyens to make major changes to Great Dixter, which at that time was in a poor state of repair. His main task was to clear the house of later alterations, and the work was undertaken with great sensitivity. But Lutyens didn't stop there. While all the restoration plans were beginning to take shape he and Nathaniel Lloyd seized on the opportunity to improve and enlarge the house. A complete timber-framed yeoman's hall at Benenden in Kent, scheduled for demolition, was skilfully dismantled and moved to Great Dixter, adding an entire wing to the house.

One of Great Dixter's most striking features is the magnificent Great Hall, the largest surviving timber-framed hall in the country. The half-timbered and plastered front and the Tudor porch also catch the eye. The contents of Great Dixter date mainly from the 17th and 18th centuries and were collected over the years by Nathaniel Lloyd. The house also contains many examples of delicately fashioned needlework, which were completed by his wife Daisy and their children.

A tour of Great Dixter doesn't end with the house: the gardens are equally impressive. Christopher Lloyd spent many years working on this project, incorporating many medieval buildings, establishing natural ponds and designing yew topiary. The result is one of the most exciting, colourful and constantly changing gardens of modern times. As with the house, plans were drawn up to improve the gardens, and here Lutyens was just as inventive. He often used tiles in a decorative though practical manner, to great effect. At Great Dixter he took a chicken house with crumbling walls and transformed it into an open-sided loggia, supported by laminated tile pillars.

The walk begins in Northiam, and heads round the edge of the village before reaching the house at Great Dixter. Even out of season, when the place is closed, you gain a vivid impression of the house and its setting. Passing directly in front of Great Dixter, the route then crosses rolling countryside to join the Sussex Border Path, following it all the way back to Northiam.

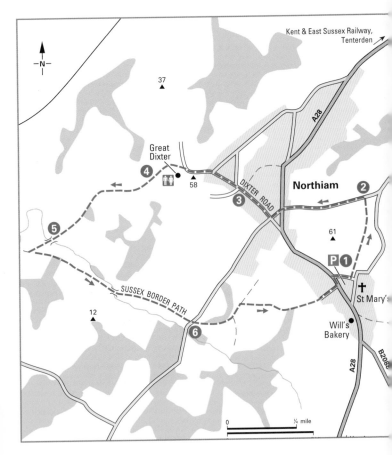

1. Turn right out of the car park and walk along Fullers Lane towards St Mary's Church. Take the path on the left, signposted to Goddens Gill, and keep to the right edge of the field. Go through a gate in the corner; away to the right you can see an oasthouse. Make for a path on the far side of the field and follow it between fences towards a thatched cottage.

2. Go through a gate and turn left to follow the road to the A28. Bear diagonally left across the A28 and follow Thyssel Lane, signposted 'Great Dixter'. Turn right at the crossroads, following Dixter Road.

3. Pass roads called Chapel Field and Higham Lane on the left, and continue to follow the signs for Great Dixter. Disregard a turning on the right (Dixter Lane) and go straight on, following a path between trees and hedges, parallel to and on the right side of the main drive to the house.

4. Pass the toilets and go between two oaks to a cattle grid. Cross the stile just to the left of it and follow the path, signposted 'Quentin's Way'. Follow the waymarks and keep left along the hedge. Go through a kissing gate in the field corner and then head diagonally down the field slope to the next kissing gate. Follow the clear path down the field slope in line with the left-hand pylon in the distance.

5. At the bottom of the field, head right for a footbridge and then turn left to join the Sussex Border Path. The path skirts the field before disappearing left into some woodland. Emerging from the trees, cut straight across the next field to a footbridge. Keep the woodland on the left and look for a gap in the trees to your left. Cross a stream to a kissing gate and then bear right. Follow the right edge of the field and keep on the Sussex Border Path until you reach the road.

6. Cross over the lane to a drive. Bear immediately left and follow the path to a stile. Pass alongside woodland and then veer slightly away from the trees to a gap in the boundary (Northiam church spire is now visible ahead). Go slightly left on the path up the field slope. Take the first footpath on the right and follow it to a gap in the field corner. Cross a footbridge under the trees and continue along the right-hand edge of the next field to join a drive. Bear left and follow it to the A28. Cross over to return to the car park at Northiam.

Where to eat and drink

On the main road in Northiam, Will's Bakery has a tea room. When Great Dixter is open, refreshments are available from an open-sided loggia and include filled baguettes, salad pots and cakes, all from a local delicatessen. There is also a picnic area.

What to see

Walk briefly off the route to visit Northiam's parish church, part of which dates from the 12th century. Most of the chancel is modern. Have a look at the clock, which was restored through the generosity of parishioners. A victory peal of bells rang out on 8 May 1945 (VE Day), and the names of the six bellringers are recorded inside the church.

While you're there

Travel a mile (1.6km) or so along the A28 to ride on the delightful Kent and East Sussex Railway. The railway, which opened in 1900, ran from Robertsbridge to Headcorn and was used for taking farm produce to market, and for bringing in coal to drive machinery and for household fires. The coalyard at the station is still in use. The line closed to passengers in 1954, and to goods in 1961. Northiam station reopened in 1990 through the efforts of the *Challenge Anneka* television show.

BATTLE – BRITAIN'S MOST FAMOUS BATTLEFIELD

DISTANCE/TIME	5 miles (8km) / 2hrs 30min
ASCENT/GRADIENT	448ft (137m) / ▲
PATHS	Field and woodland paths, some road walking, several stiles
LANDSCAPE	Gently undulating farmland and woodland
SUGGESTED MAP	OS Explorer 124 Hastings & Bexhill
START/FINISH	Grid reference: TQ747156
DOG FRIENDLINESS	Enclosed woodland paths and stretches of 1066 Country Walk suitable for dogs off lead
PARKING	English Heritage car park at Battle Abbey (fee charged)
PUBLIC TOILETS	Mount Street car park in Battle; Battle Abbey

One of the most important and significant events of the last millennium, the 1066 Battle of Hastings represents a defining moment in British history. Visit the battlefield and you can still sense something of that momentous day when William, Duke of Normandy, defeated Harold and his Saxon army and became William the Conqueror of England. See the spot where Harold is believed to have fallen and, with a little imagination, you can picture the bloody events that led to his defeat.

William began by occupying a position on a hill about 400yds (365m) to the south of the English army, massed on a higher hilltop. Harold and his men fortified their formidable position and, following abortive uphill charges on the English shield-wall, the Normans withdrew, unable to breach the defences. It looked for a time as if victory was within Harold's grasp until William rallied his men and executed two successful strategies. One was to instruct his bowmen to shoot their arrows indiscriminately into the air, though William had no idea that one of them would (so one version of the tale says) hit Harold in the eye, fatally wounding him. William's other plan was to create the impression that his armies were fleeing the battlefield. Sensing victory, the English gave chase, but this was to be their downfall. The Normans rounded on them and won the battle.

William marched victoriously to London where he was crowned King of England. Before the Battle of Hastings, William had vowed that if God gave him victory, he would build an abbey on the site of the battle at Senlac Hill. This he did, with the high altar set up on the spot where Harold died. The abbey, thought to have been completed before William died, was significantly enlarged and improved over the years that followed. However, after the Dissolution of the Monasteries, much of it was converted into a private house by Sir Anthony Browne, Henry VIII's Master of Horse. Battle Abbey is now in the care of English Heritage. This walk begins in the centre of Battle, so allow time before or after the walk to visit the abbey and its historic battlefield.

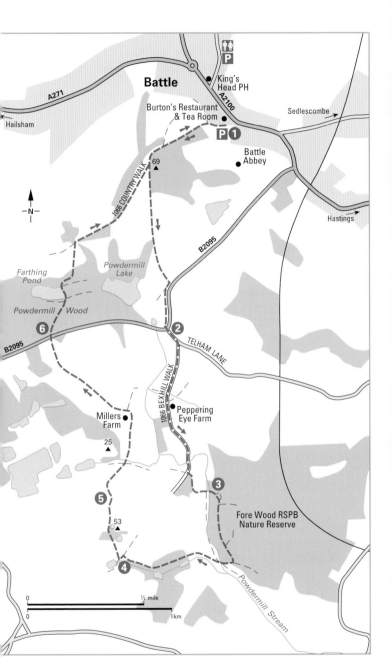

1. Turn left out of the car park and follow the track to a gate. Keep left along the bridleway beside woodland, the path swinging left to a fingerpost and junction of paths. Bear left with the 1066 Bexhill Walk marker and walk down the field-edge and through two gates. Keep ahead, soon to cross a drive via two gates, and follow the fenced path along the field-edge high above the road.

2. Cross the B2095 (take care: dangerous bend), walk along Telham Lane and take the private road right towards Peppering Eye Farm. After the farm, keep to the metalled drive for 0.5 miles (0.8km), passing under power cables and crossing a stream to ascend to a junction of paths by Powdermill Cottage. Turn left along a track through the trees to a gate, and bear left with the waymarker across a field.

3. Cross a footbridge to enter Fore Wood RSPB Nature Reserve. Bear right and follow the yellow-arrowed route through the wood, ignoring a path on the left and turning right at the far side of the wood where the path curves left at a bench. Go left at the fingerpost, cross a footbridge and follow the path right through scrub, parallel with the stream. On reaching an open field, keep left around the field-edge to leave at the top left corner. Cross a track and carry on along an overgrown and rough path in a wooded area, past a pond that is just about visible down to the left. This passes another larger pond, then soon emerges into a field; keep going straight ahead along the field-edge.

4. Reach a junction of tracks and bear left, then immediately right at a fork, curving left around a pond to emerge from the woodland by pheasant pens. Turn right up a grassy unwaymarked track 20yds (18m) before the pens. Soon enter woodland and continue to a footbridge. Turn left to a stile, then right along the field-edge passing a pond, and head across the field in line with distant barns, passing beneath power cables.

5. Beyond the next gateway, bear diagonally right downhill across the field to a gate and go forward up a track. Just before the barns, climb the stile on the right to follow the arrowed path around Millers Farm to reach a gate just before the brick farmhouse. Rejoin the track and follow it for 0.5 miles (0.8km).

6. Cross a road, pass beside a gate and follow the path through Powdermill Wood. Cross a footbridge and go along a fence by Farthing Pond, at the end of which fork left uphill along a narrow path through woodland to a kissing gate. Cross the field, aiming to the right of a cottage to reach another kissing gate. Turn right along a track, go through a gate and follow the 1066 Country Walk uphill through a field. Retrace your outward route back to the car park.

Where to eat and drink

There are several pubs, restaurants and tea rooms in Battle, including the 15th-century King's Head, Burton's Restaurant &Tea Room, and the Battle Deli and Coffee Shop.

What to see

Fore Wood RSPB Nature Reserve is home to dragonflies, damselflies, nuthatches, treecreepers and woodpeckers, with rare mosses and ferns thriving in the shaded valleys.

While you're there

Pay a visit to Battle Abbey. After exploring the ruins of the former Benedictine monastery you can drop in on the new gatehouse exhibition, which examines the abbey's pivotal role in English history. Climb to the roof to enjoy arguably the best views of the battlefield.

BURWASH – RUDYARD KIPLING'S HOME

DISTANCE/TIME	4.75 miles (7.7km) / 2hrs
ASCENT/GRADIENT	345ft (105m) / ▲ ▲ ▲
PATHS	Field and woodland paths, stretches of minor road, several stiles
LANDSCAPE	Rolling, semi-wooded countryside of the Dudwell Valley
SUGGESTED MAPS	OS Explorer 136 High Weald
START/FINISH	Grid reference: TQ674246
DOG FRIENDLINESS	Dogs on lead in vicinity of Bateman's and Park Farm and on stretches of farmland. Off lead on woodland paths and tracks. Bateman's is dog friendly but has a few rules it asks dog owners to abide by.
PARKING	Free car park off A265 in Burwash village
PUBLIC TOILETS	At car park

Bateman's, in the village of Burwash, was Rudyard Kipling's refuge. This was his spiritual home, and it was here that he found true happiness. Touring the house and exploring the garden, it's not difficult to see why he fell in love with the place. It is a charming family home, small and intimate, occupying a peaceful setting in a secluded valley. Built by a local ironmaster in 1634, the house lies about 25 miles (40km) to the northeast of Kipling's old home at Rottingdean. Kipling purchased the house in 1902 and, now in the care of the National Trust, it remains much as it was in Kipling's day.

It was here, in his book-lined study, that Kipling wrote some of his most famous works, including *Puck of Pook's Hill*. The house and the tranquillity of the surrounding countryside greatly inspired him, and over the years he acquired more land so that he could write and relax away from public scrutiny; 'We have loved it ever since our first sight of it', he wrote later. Kipling loved the garden just as much as the house, designing and landscaping it and putting his own mark on it. He planted yew hedges to give him more privacy, and even erected a pear arch. Visitors to Bateman's can see the results of his labours, and they can also take a stroll through the beautiful rose garden, which he designed after being awarded the Nobel Prize for Literature in 1907.

Kipling was not a recluse and liked to socialise, but he was known for his rather curious but discreet manner of asking guests to leave. He would lead them past the garden sundial, which indicated that it was later than it really was, and he would then suggest that they should make their farewells. He was a keen motorist too. He bought a Rolls-Royce and embarked on many journeys, travelling abroad and visiting his old school in Devon. He recorded his travels in detail, and even dispatched reports and memos to the Automobile Association. This glorious valley walk passes Bateman's near the start and then again towards the finish, enabling you to choose when you go there to visit. A tour of the house and gardens reveals how the National Trust has preserved the character and integrity of the man, as well as the atmosphere of the place. Kipling died in 1936, after 34 years at Bateman's. Looking at the house today, it is not difficult to see why he described it as 'a real house in which to settle down for keeps... a good and peaceable place'.

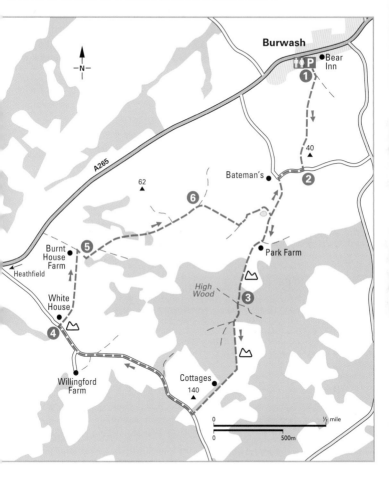

1. Make for the footpath behind the toilet block. Follow the path down the slope and, at a junction of paths, cross the plank bridge and gate on the right. Continue ahead, making for the next gate, and keep the boundary hedge on your right. Pass through another gate and then head diagonally down the field. Make for a gap in the field corner, follow the left-hand field-edge to a stile and exit to the road. (Make a mental note of this point, as you will return to it later.)

2. Turn right and follow the lane along to Bateman's. Keep left in front of the house itself and proceed past some other houses. At Park Farm ignore the

arrowed gate on the left and continue through the farm, then bear left uphill, through the edge of some woodland to a gate. Head up the field slope, keeping the trees on your immediate right. Look for a gate and bridleway post on the right, passing through the wood.

3. Bear left at a T-junction with a track, then immediately right, and follow the bridleway, keeping left at the fork. Pass a pair of remote cottages and walk along to the road. Turn right, eventually passing the entrance to Willingford Farm and then, after the road crosses a stream, start to climb quite steeply.

4. Just before a small white house on the right, go right through a kissing gate. After a stile, climb a narrow path that tends to become clogged with nettles and brambles in summer. Head diagonally across a large field; soon the buildings of Burnt House Farm come into view. Go through a small metal gate (the left-hand of two gates) in the field corner, carry on below the buildings through waymarked gates, then walk along the top left side of a field.

5. At a junction of waymarked paths keep forward, ignoring the path to the right. Carry on along the edge of the next field, past a metal water tank and down through a belt of woodland to a field, and head down just to left of the chimney of a house. Turn right along a surfaced lane which very quickly becomes a grassy track, passing some dilapidated farm outbuildings.

6. Cross over a stile by a gate and keep right. Look for a galvanised gate near the end of the field, turn left and then skirt round the edge of the field. Veer over to a stile towards the far end, cross a footbridge and turn left. Follow the path over a sluice, past a pond and a cottage, bearing right to a track. Turn left and head back to Bateman's, and retrace your steps to Burwash.

Where to eat and drink
The Bear Inn, next to the car park at Burwash, has been in business for more than 300 years. It serves bar meals and restaurant food. The village is also home to the Rose and Crown, which serves Harvey's beers from Lewes. In addition, Burwash has the Lime Tree Tea Rooms. Bateman's includes a popular tea room.

What to see
Neighbouring Bateman's is the picturesque village of Burwash, which lies on a ridge between the rivers Rother and Dudwell. There are many white weatherboarded cottages and various beautiful tile-hung buildings, making it typical of East Sussex. The war memorial by the church was unveiled by Rudyard Kipling, and his son is one of those commemorated. The church has a fine Norman tower with a shingled spire.

While you're there
If you have time, make a point of visiting the watermill at Bateman's. The 18th-century mill, which was restored by dedicated volunteers, grinds corn for flour, and attached to the wheel is one of the earliest water-driven turbines, installed by Rudyard Kipling to generate electricity for the house. There is a delightful walk from the house to the watermill on the River Dudwell.

BRIGHTLING'S FOLLY TRAIL

DISTANCE/TIME	5 miles (8km) / 2hrs 30min
ASCENT/GRADIENT	197ft (60m) / ▲
PATHS	Parkland paths, woodland bridleways and lanes, three stiles
LANDSCAPE	Parkland and dense woodland
SUGGESTED MAP	OS Explorer 124 Hastings & Bexhill
START/FINISH	Grid reference: TQ683210
DOG FRIENDLINESS	Off lead in woodland, but heed signs
PARKING	Limited spaces by phone box near Brightling church. Avoid times of church services. Alternatively, park at Darwell
PUBLIC TOILETS	None on route

Scattered around the peaceful village of Brightling are the monuments and follies created by former resident John 'Mad Jack' Fuller – a man for whom the description 'eccentric' is something of an understatement. Long after Fuller's death in 1834, his name lives on, as does his reputation as a wilful, autocratic and larger-than-life character who embraced a wide range of interests and became a renowned patron of the arts.

John Fuller was born in 1757, the son of a Hampshire rector. The family made its money from the Sussex iron industry, allowing the young John a privileged upbringing. He attended Eton and on his 20th birthday inherited the family fortune and its estates. His future was secure. He came close to marriage in his 30s, but his proposal was declined. Fuller remained a bachelor for the rest of his life, at first throwing himself headlong into politics. He stood for Parliament on several occasions and eventually became the Honourable Member for East Sussex. But Fuller was no ordinary MP. He was the stuff of which legends are made, swearing at the Speaker of the House of Commons, thundering down from London in a carriage with footmen armed to the teeth with pistols and drawn swords, refusing a peerage, consuming three bottles of port a day and engaging in reckless, impossible wagers. It was hardly surprising that he became known as 'Mad Jack'.

With his 22-stone (140kg) frame and loud, bellowing voice, Fuller often induced fear in the strongest of souls. In fact, his quick temper and unpredictable nature eventually ruined his prospects of climbing the political ladder. After insulting the Speaker he was forcibly removed from the chamber, and ordered to apologise. He did not stand again for Parliament and became disillusioned with politics, instead focusing his attention on folly-building.

Explore Brightling and the surrounding countryside and you will see Fuller's follies everywhere, reflecting his taste for the absurd. Even his final resting place seems wildly over the top. This, his final folly, is a sandstone pyramid mausoleum erected in Brightling churchyard, where the walk begins.

For many years people genuinely believed that Fuller had been interred in an upright position, dressed for dinner, holding a bottle of claret and wearing a top hat. When the tomb was eventually opened for restoration work, the rumours proved to be unfounded – though, given his exuberant personality, it would not have been surprising if the gossip had proved true.

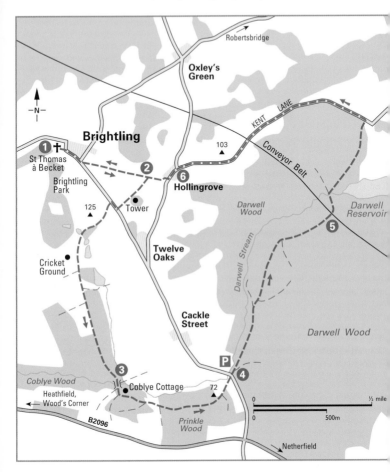

1. Enter the churchyard opposite Wealden House and walk through it, down to the road. Turn right to reach Brightling Park and make for a turning on the left, signposted 'Robertsbridge'. Go through a galvanised kissing gate by the junction and follow the path along the fence, through a kissing gate and across a small field. Go forward between a hedge and a fence to a footpath junction and sign.

2. Turn right here over a stile and follow the field-edge towards the tower. Cross a stile on the right, cut through the trees past the tower and descend the field slope to the stile and road. Bear right for a few paces, turning left by the barns and outbuildings of Ox Lodge. Cut between ponds and lakes and look for a cricket ground by the track. The temple can be glimpsed on the hill behind

the pavilion. Pass a turning to some farm outbuildings and continue on the main bridleway, signed 'Coblye', keeping straight ahead when it forks. Cut through an area of pheasant-rearing woodland and descend.

3. Cross a footbridge, climb past Coblye Cottage on the left, then fork left and keep to the main track through Prinkle Wood, ignoring paths left and right. Eventually reach a waymarker post and gate, exit the wood and follow the track downhill to a gate and road. Cross over.

4. From the car park, with the road behind you, take the left-hand bridle track and, when it eventually forks, keep to the right. When the track rises and then swings to the right at a long hairpin bend, turn left and follow the unwaymarked path downhill through the wood, keeping right when it levels out and is joined by a path from the left. Do the same thing a little further on, now walking parallel to a signed bridleway with which the path merges.

5. On emerging from the trees, cross over a pipe enclosing a conveyor belt linking Mountfield and Brightling gypsum mines. Follow the track to the left and then veer right after a few steps at the fork. Cross over the Darwell Stream and bear right, following the woodland path up through the trees to the road. Turn right to glimpse Darwell Reservoir and turn left to continue the walk. Follow Kent Lane, recross the conveyor belt and make for the hamlet of Hollingrove. On the right here is an old chapel, which is now a house.

6. Keep left at the junction and walk along the lane for a short distance, passing Whitehouse. Take the stony track on the right and veer left after a few paces in front of a part tile-hung house (AEF 1840 on the front). Walk along to the turning for the tower, visited near the start of the walk, then retrace your steps across the fields and follow the road back to Brightling church.

Where to eat and drink
While there is nowhere to seek refreshment on the route, the nearby village of Netherfield, to the southeast of this walk, has two pubs: the White Hart and the Netherfield Arms, both of which serve food.

What to see
In the middle of Brightling Park, landscaped by 'Capability' Brown, stands the Grecian-style Rotunda Temple, a circular domed building. It may have been used as a hideout for smugglers or a store for contraband. Darwell Reservoir is managed as a trout fishery and is popular with anglers and ornithologists.

While you're there
Have a look at the pyramid mausoleum and step inside the parish church. John Fuller was a generous benefactor, and his donations included a barrel organ in 1820. Near the start of the walk is one of Fuller's more accessible follies. The circular tower, which dates to the 1820s, is a two-storey, stone construction with a Gothic entrance and battlements. Some sources suggest that Fuller erected it so he could see Bodiam Castle, which he later bought to save it from demolition.

HISTORY AND SCIENCE AT HERSTMONCEUX

DISTANCE/TIME	3 miles (4.8km) / 1hr 30min
ASCENT/GRADIENT	153ft (47m) / ▲
PATHS	Woodland and field paths, country lanes
LANDSCAPE	Wood, farmland and parkland on edge of Pevensey Levels
SUGGESTED MAP	OS Explorer 124 Hastings & Bexhill
START/FINISH	Grid reference: TQ654103
DOG FRIENDLINESS	On lead in woodland. Off lead on 1066 Country Walk
PARKING	Small lay-by on Wartling Road, south of A271, near entrance to the Observatory Science Centre
PUBLIC TOILETS	Castle and Science Centre, seasonal opening (visitors only)

A romantic-looking 15th-century moated castle set in beautiful parkland and superb Elizabethan gardens, Herstmonceux perfectly captures the essence of medieval England, although it is actually inspired by the French chateaux of the period. At the time William, Duke of Normandy marched through Sussex to do battle with Harold and his Saxon army, Herstmonceux was probably no more than a small manor. Herst is a Saxon word meaning 'clearing', and Monceux comes from Drogo de Monceux, a relative of William.

The land later passed to the Fiennes family, ancestors of Ralph Fiennes and his brother Joseph, two of Britain's leading contemporary actors. It was in 1441 that Sir Roger de Fiennes, treasurer of the royal household, applied for a royal licence to build a castle here – though he wanted to use it to entertain his friends, not to defend his country. When first erected it was the only building in England of its size to be formed of bricks. Herstmonceux is also perhaps the first example of a 'sham' – a country pile disguised as a castle. Much of the interior was demolished in 1776 to build nearby Herstmonceux Place, which is glimpsed from a distance on this walk, and which from 1807 to 1819 was the residence of Thomas Read Kemp, the founder of Kemptown in Brighton.

By Victorian times, the castle was little more than a romantic ruin. Herstmonceux Castle was rebuilt in 1911, and in 1947 it became the home of the Royal Greenwich Observatory, which had been established on the east side of London in 1646 under Charles II, with the purpose of recording the position of the stars as a navigation aid to sailors. Due to increasing light pollution, the observatory relocated again in 1984, this time to the top of an extinct volcano on La Palma in the Canary Islands. The castle and grounds were bought by Queen's University, Ontario, for use as an international study centre, a role that continues to this day. During late August, the whole site is transformed by a huge medieval festival featuring knights in armour, falconry displays, jousting tournaments, strolling minstrels and jesters. In sharp contrast to the castle are the buildings of the Observatory Science Centre next door. These famous green domes still house large telescopes, and it is possible to come on open evenings and see the night sky close up.

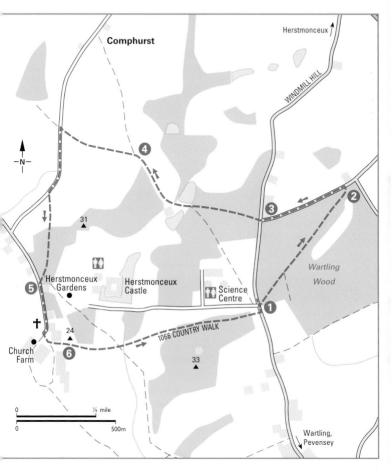

1. From the lay-by, make for the entrance to the Science Centre, cross Wartling Road to a stile and enter the extensive woodland. Turn left at a T-junction by a signpost and continue on the straight footpath, picking your way through the trees.

2. Eventually you will reach a stile. Turn left, then immediately left again onto Wood Lane. Follow the road, with the coppiced woodland and an ancient boundary bank seen on the left.

3. Reach a road junction and cross over to a signposted bridleway. Continue ahead through the woodland on a path that is initially concrete. Just after a path joins from the left, pass a reed-clogged lake (one of a chain of ponds), and carry on along the wide path between the trees.

4. Emerge into farmland by a galvanised gate, with a view of 18th-century Herstmonceux Place. Turn left along a track across the field, then turn left again at a junction of tracks, before forking right to go through a gate. Veer left at a waymark by a concrete trough. Cross the field, heading up the slope to reach a line of trees. Look for a gate, avoid the immediate fork to the left, and follow the level path through the woodland. Cross over a path and then continue walking along the bridleway.

5. Reach the road and turn left. Just past Herstmonceux church, turn left on the 1066 Country Walk and follow the concrete drive to a gate to the left of the entrance to Church Farm House.

6. Cross over a tarmac lane serving the study centre and, as you descend the slope, the domes of the old observatory begin to peep into view just above the trees. Make for the next galvanised gate and an impressive view of Herstmonceux Castle over on the left. Cross a footpath to another gate. Begin a gradual, though not particularly steep, climb and continue on the 1066 Country Walk as it runs hard by the Science Centre boundary. Follow the woodland path to the road, turn left and return to the lay-by.

Where to eat and drink
The Lamb Inn at nearby Wartling is an attractive 17th-century free house and restaurant. There is a tea room in the grounds of Herstmonceux Castle and plenty of picnic space at the Science Centre and Discovery Park.

What to see
Herstmonceux church, about 2 miles (3.2km) from the village centre and overlooking Pevensey Levels, stands on a wooded rise opposite one of the entrances to Herstmonceux Castle. The church is dedicated to All Saints, indicating that it is probably of Saxon origin. As you join the 1066 Country Walk, you cannot fail to spot the white-domed satellite laser ranger, which belongs to the Royal Greenwich Observatory.

While you're there
Visit the grounds of Herstmonceux Castle to see the walled garden (from before 1570), a herb garden, woodland sculptures and a folly. Walks take you to the remains of a 300-year-old sweet chestnut avenue, a rhododendron garden and a waterfall. The castle itself is sometimes open for guided tours, and you can stop off at the Observatory Science Centre, where astronomy exhibitions illustrate the work and history of the observatory.

ROMANS AND NORMANS AT PEVENSEY LEVELS

DISTANCE/TIME	4.5 miles (7.2km) / 1hr 45min
ASCENT/GRADIENT	Negligible
PATHS	Field paths and riverside, brief stretch of road, two stiles
LANDSCAPE	Low-level former marshland, flat and watery landscape
SUGGESTED MAP	AA Walker's Map 30 Eastbourne & Beachy Head
START/FINISH	Grid reference: TQ645048
DOG FRIENDLINESS	Under control on farmland and minor roads
PARKING	Pay-and-display car park by Pevensey Castle
PUBLIC TOILETS	At car park

The great harbour here silted up long ago, leaving Pevensey stranded inland, 2 miles (3.2km) from the sea. It was from here that William, Duke of Normandy, marched inland to defeat King Harold and his Saxon army in 1066 at the Battle of Hastings – to this day one of the most significant events in English history. The exact spot where William came ashore can now never be identified, as the coastline has shifted and altered so greatly down the centuries since then. What is known, however, is that 800 years before the arrival of William, the Romans had chosen this site to construct the fortress of Anderida as part of their defence of the Saxon Shore. Pevensey was one of a series of fortifications along this coast, and the remains of the outer walls of the castle survive. Standing up to 30ft (9m) thick in places and enclosing an oval area of about 10 acres (4ha), the walls are considered to be among the finest surviving examples of Roman building in England.

Determined to claim the English crown, William expected to be met with some resistance at Anderida. But he found the fort undefended, enabling him to consolidate his position immediately. Harold and his men were elsewhere, fighting his brother's Danish army in Yorkshire and expecting William to sail via the Isle of Wight. The Normans immediately set about erecting one of three prefabricated timber castles they had brought with them, constructing it on a mound of earth within the fort. It was as if they were intent on taking the place of the Romans who had occupied this site so many years before them. Without opposition, the Norman army travelled almost casually through the Sussex countryside, taking food from local people and burning and looting whatever they could find along the way.

Following his victory at the Battle of Hastings, William gave the stronghold to his half-brother, Robert, Count of Mortain. It was Robert who built the Norman castle, the remains of which we can still see there today. A keep and bailey were subsequently constructed, and in the 13th century a formidable stone curtain wall and gatehouse were added. Further work took place in the

14th century, but by now the castle was sturdy enough to defend itself and its inhabitants from the strongest opponent.

Pevensey was prepared to defend the coast from the threat of Napoleon and, even as recently as 1940, pill boxes were installed in the castle walls in case German forces should invade. This atmospheric walk starts at Pevensey Castle. After a brief tour of Pevensey, with its picturesque houses and cottages, head out across the lonely, evocative Pevensey Levels, once covered by water and now reminiscent of the fenland country of East Anglia.

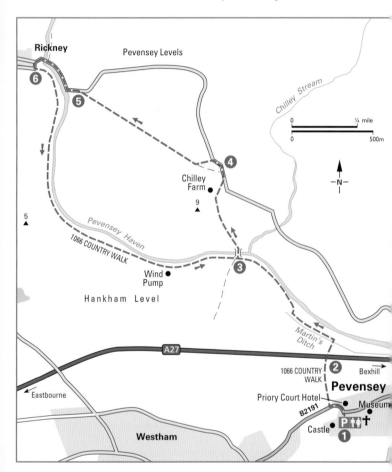

1. Walk from the car park to the main street, keeping forward on the bend past the castle entrance and the Priory Court Hotel. Pevensey Castle's walls rise up impressively on your left. Bear off to the right just beyond the hotel and a house called The Gables to follow the 1066 Country Walk.

2. Cross the A27 with care and keep on the trail. Go through a gate and follow the path as it bends left. Continue between fencing and hedging, alongside Martin's Ditch on the left, until you pass through a galvanised gate. Bear right

to the riverbank, turn left alongside the Pevensey Haven and saunter past its confluence with the Chilley Stream.

3. Continue for a short distance to a footbridge. Cross over it and then aim diagonally towards a footbridge to the right of a house. Carry on across the next field to a stile and footbridge. Bear diagonally right to a wooden gate, then turn right and walk along the track to the road, passing Chilley Farm Shop.

4. Turn left at the lane, and where it bends right go ahead through a gate. Soon reach two gates, and go through the right-hand one. Keep ahead alongside a drainage ditch to a gate in the field corner and continue, keeping the ditch on your left. Make for a footbridge on the left. Cross it and bear right (sharper than indicated by the waymarker) alongside the ditch. Follow the ditch to a stile by a galvanised gate with a road beyond.

5. Turn left along the road and walk along to the hamlet of Rickney. Avoid the 1066 Country Walk as it runs off to the right, and cross the little road bridge. Bear left into Rickney Road at the sign for Hankham and immediately cross a bridge.

6. Turn left after a few paces through a gate and follow the 1066 Country Walk, pass beside a barn to reach a galvanised gate and continue ahead to the right of a pylon along the right-hand field-edge, soon to reach the Pevensey Haven on your left. Continue beside the river. Pass a wind pump and the footbridge crossed earlier and then retrace your steps to the A27 and Pevensey.

Where to eat and drink
Chilley Farm Shop serves tea, coffee, ploughmans', cream teas and a range of tasty sandwiches and cakes. The Royal Oak & Castle Inn and the Smugglers also serve food; soft drinks are sold at the castle shop. You'll also find the Cottage Castle Tearoom right next to the car park.

What to see
A former coastal inlet that was drained mainly in the 14th and 15th centuries, the Pevensey Levels have their own individual character. This is a haven for wildlife, plants and insects, as well as home to a great variety of birds, both in summer and winter. Redshank, plovers, snipe and wildfowl visit in winter, while skylarks and kestrels are found here throughout the year.

While you're there
Take a stroll through the ancient town of Pevensey and visit the fascinating Court House Museum in the High Street, once the smallest town hall in England. In 1882, under the Municipal Corporation Act, Pevensey lost its status as a borough, and in 1890 the Pevensey Town Trust was established to administer the Court House. Inside, you can see the Court Room, Robing Room, cells and exercise yard. There are many exhibits and displays, including a silver penny of William I minted at Pevensey.

BIRLING GAP
TO BEACHY HEAD

DISTANCE/TIME	7 miles (11.2km) / 3hrs
ASCENT/GRADIENT	536ft (163m) / ▲ ▲
PATHS	Downland paths and tracks, clifftop greensward
LANDSCAPE	Southern boundary of South Downs and headland
SUGGESTED MAP	AA Walker's Map 30 Eastbourne & Beachy Head
START/FINISH	Grid reference: TV554959
DOG FRIENDLINESS	On lead by Cornish Farm and on South Downs Way
PARKING	Pay-and-display National Trust car park at Birling Gap
PUBLIC TOILETS	Birling Gap and Beachy Head

The magnificent chalk cliffs of Beachy Head were formed from the shells of billions of minute creatures which fell to the bottom of a subtropical sea. Today, this stretch of coast is one of Britain's most famous landmarks. The treeless South Downs reach the sea in spectacular fashion, and over 500ft (152m) below the towering cliffs lies Beachy Head's distinctive red and white lighthouse, standing alone on a remote beach. This blend of natural and artificial features creates a magnificent picture. The present 142ft (43m) lighthouse, automated in 1983 and modernised in 1999, has been vital to the safety of mariners off this coast since it was completed in 1902. But even as far back as 1670 a beacon shone from this point, helping to guide ships away from the treacherous ledges below.

Beachy Head has always been a navigational nightmare. Sailors have long feared it, and the Venetians dubbed it the Devil's Cape. In 1831 the Sussex landowner John Fuller built the Belle Tout lighthouse high up on the headland to the west of Beachy Head. The lamp was first lit in 1834, but the lighthouse was never a great success. Its lofty position on the cliff top meant that it was often shrouded in mist and fog and therefore invisible to shipping in the English Channel. A decision was eventually taken to erect a lighthouse at sea level.

The name Beachy Head comes from the Norman French *beau chef*, meaning beautiful headland. The description is certainly apt, and this breezy, sprawling cliff top draws visitors and tourists from far and wide who come to marvel at the breathtaking sea views or saunter along the South Downs Way. The whole area is a designated Site of Special Scientific Interest (SSSI). The walk begins at Birling Gap to the west of Beachy Head. Before long it heads inland, running across the slopes of the South Downs. Within sight of Eastbourne, it suddenly switches direction, following the South Downs Way to Beachy Head and back to Birling Gap. On the way it passes the old Belle Tout lighthouse, now a bed and breakfast establishment.

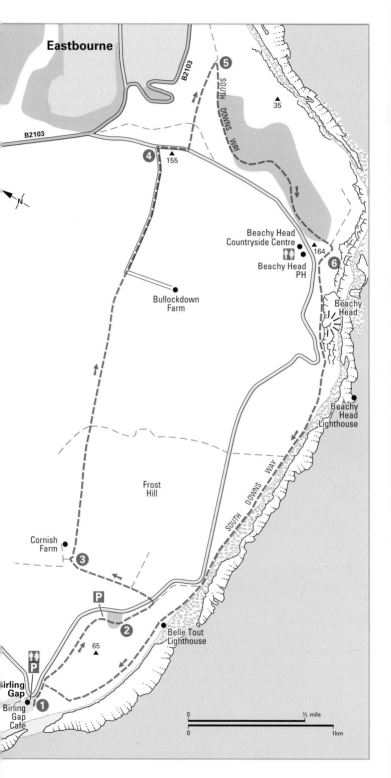

Eastbourne

B2103

SOUTH DOWNS WAY

⑤

▲ 35

B2103

④

▲ 155

N

Beachy Head
Countryside Centre ●
🚻 ●

Beachy Head
PH

▲ 164

⑥

Beachy
Head

Bullockdown
Farm ●

Beachy
Head
Lighthouse ●

Frost
Hill

SOUTH DOWNS WAY

Cornish
Farm ┤
③

P

②

Belle Tout
Lighthouse ●

▲ 65

P
🚻

irling
Gap

① ●

Birling
Gap
Café

0 ———————— ½ mile
0 ———————— 1km

43

1. Facing the cottages in the car park, take the leftmost track, by a parking ticket machine near the car park entrance, and parallel to the road. Keep to the right of the next car park and follow the path between the trees.

2. A few paces after emerging from the trees, look for a junction with a concrete track on the other side of the road; take the next left path to meet it. Follow the bridleway signposted 'East Dean Down'. Glance back for a view of the old Belle Tout lighthouse. Pass a fingerpost and continue ahead.

3. Follow the concrete track as it bends right towards Cornish Farm, avoiding the faint grass path going straight on. Just before the farm and some pens, go right through a waymarked gate and shortly afterwards another, and walk along the spine of the ridge, keeping the fence on your right-hand side. Make for another gate and continue straight ahead. Pass alongside lines of bushes before reaching the next gate. To the right you will see Bullockdown Farm, and fields and pastures enclosed by flint walls.

4. Pass beside a barrier to the road and turn right, following the wide grassy verge. On reaching two adjoining barriers and the end of a wall on the right, cross the road and take a path through grassland to a five-way junction, bearing half left down a broad grassy track. At the next junction, fork right at the signpost (left is the South Downs Way).

5. 100yds (91m) later, as you come to a single tree on your left, turn sharp right on the South Downs Way (ahead is signposted to the seafront) and follow the long-distance trail as it climbs steadily between bushes and vegetation. Keep right when another path comes in from the left, and contour round the slopes, eventually reaching a tarmac path just above an RAF memorial and a viewpoint of Beachy Head lighthouse at the foot of the cliff. Cross the grass, up the slope. In front of you now are the Beachy Head Pub and Beachy Head Countryside Centre.

6. Return to the South Downs Way and follow it downhill, with the sea on your left. The path can be seen ahead, running over the undulating cliff top. Keep the Belle Tout lighthouse in your sights and follow the path up towards it. Keep to the right of the old lighthouse and soon the car park at Birling Gap edges into view, as do the famous Seven Sisters cliffs. Carry on down, finally dropping to the right to return to the car park.

Where to eat and drink
Birling Gap has a National Trust café. The Beachy Head pub has a bar and restaurant. It gets very busy on summer days and bank holidays.

What to see
By the wooden railings where you first see Beachy Head Lighthouse is a memorial to the 110,000 members of RAF Bomber Command. The hill on which Belle Tout Lighthouse stands has a prehistoric ditch running its length, thought to be of late neolithic or early Bronze Age origins.

While you're there
Beachy Head Countryside Centre is both educational and entertaining. The centre illustrates the history of the area and its coastline.

NEOLITHIC DOWNLANDS AROUND JEVINGTON

DISTANCE/TIME	3 miles (4.8km) / 1hr 45min
ASCENT/GRADIENT	420ft (122m) / ▲ ▲
PATHS	Downland tracks and field paths with a short stretch of lane in Jevington village, several stiles
LANDSCAPE	Up high on the South Downs, mainly grassland with long views and deep-cut combes
SUGGESTED MAP	AA Walker's Map 30 Eastbourne & Beachy Head
START/FINISH	Grid reference: TQ579017
DOG FRIENDLINESS	On lead towards Combe Hill on the northern leg of the route among grazing sheep
PARKING	Butts Brow pay-and-display car park, accessed via Willingdon off the A22
PUBLIC TOILETS	None on route

Around the crest of Combe Hill a neolithic or New Stone Age enclosure was built on a causeway, surrounded by two concentric ditches. Such enclosures date back to before 3000 BC and there are four known in Sussex, with the Trundle above Chichester being the most famous of these. No one knows what they were used for, but informed suggestions include tribal gatherings, corralling farm animals, protection in times of danger, or for the predecessors of markets and fairs. Also on the hill are the humps of tumuli or burial mounds, and on the southern slopes ancient field systems can be picked out.

St Andrew's Church in Jevington would have more Anglo-Saxon features in evidence had the 1873 restoration been less drastic. Despite this, the tower is recognisably Anglo-Saxon and at least the ancient colonettes in the modern belfry openings are genuine ones that have been reused. You can see remnants of a blocked window lower down the tower, with arches of thin Roman bricks salvaged from somewhere else, perhaps Pevensey. The nave is also partly 11th-century, but the most famous feature is the Jevington Slab, believed to date from the 11th century, when England was ruled by Danish kings. It shows a figure of Christ in a loincloth, and writhing foliage carved in the Scandinavian 'Urnes' style. How it got here is unknown, but it was found in the tower in 1785 and is now mounted on the north wall.

A smuggler's tale

Jevington and surrounding areas were hotbeds of smuggling in the 18th century, and Alfriston, on the Cuckmere River to the west, now trades on its smuggling past. In the late 18th century James Pettit ('Jevington Jigg') led the local smugglers. He was the landlord of the inn, now The Eight Bells. One of his escapes from the excise officers was made in women's clothing, but he was eventually convicted for horse stealing and transported in 1799 to Botany Bay in Australia.

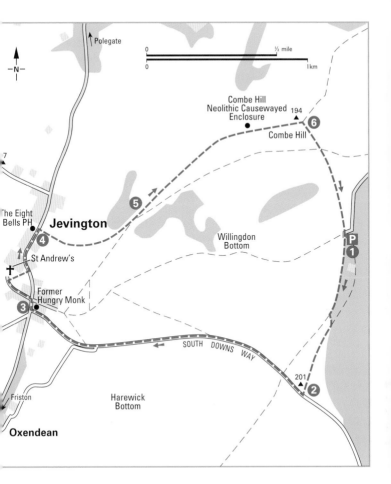

1. From the car park car head south towards Beachy Head as indicated on the stone sign block and guidepost. The deep combe of Willingdon Bottom is away to your right, then Eastbourne can be seen to your left as you steadily ascend – and, looking right, you can see Jevington church and the heavily wooded slopes behind it. Ignore a chalky path that crosses over the grassy track.

2. At the crest, now at 660ft (201m) above sea level, you reach a trig point and then soon after a footpath junction with the South Downs Way long-distance footpath. Bear right onto the Way. Go straight on at the next signpost and descend towards Jevington, the flat-bottomed dry valley of Harewick Bottom to your left and sheep grazing beyond the path's post and wire fences. Nearing Jevington, the path becomes an old hill pasture access lane.

3. When you reach Jevington, turn right onto the village street. On your right is the former Hungry Monk restaurant, where a plaque celebrates the fact that it was the birthplace of banoffee pie. The building is now private dwellings. Just past the bus stop, go left onto Church Lane. At the

churchyard leave the South Downs Way to pass to the right of the church, then continue alongside the high flint boundary wall to Jevington Place. Leaving the churchyard via a rotating timber gate known as a 'tapsel gate' and designed to assist coffin bearers, the path bears left alongside the village road to The Eight Bells pub.

4. Opposite the pub go right onto the footpath up steps. The path continues ahead, shortly climbing steadily between post and wire fences to a kissing gate. Through this go half left across sheep-cropped downland.

5. At the second guidepost, fork left up to a stile with long views north towards the Weald. Continue ahead to a gap in the scrub and over another stile pass between the gorse and thorn, beyond it continuing ahead to the summit, with its pronounced burial mound, or tumulus; its sunken top hints at previous looting by treasure-seekers. The summit is Combe Hill, flanked by a neolithic causewayed enclosure, its banks relatively clear. To the north the escarpment descends very steeply into the Combe and, if you look carefully, you'll spot Polegate Windmill rising out of its suburban surroundings.

6. After the 636ft (194m) summit, the path bears gently right, then ahead to take you back to the car park.

Where to eat and drink
In Jevington The Eight Bells pub does good food and has a beer garden with a fine view over fields.

What to see
As you climb east from Jevington between the kissing gate and the stile, you cross a series of often indiscernible banks, part of one of Sussex's finest surviving Celtic field systems, probably dating from 1000 BC. They are shown on Ordnance Survey maps as a series of narrow rectangles on the southern, sunnier, slopes of the hill, each field usually enclosing up to 2 acres (0.8ha).

While you're there
Polegate Windmill, seen from Combe Hill, is open on Sunday afternoons and bank holidays from Easter until the end of October. Off the A22, it is a brick tower mill built in 1817 and restored in 1967 as a working mill. There is a fascinating museum of milling, with working models.

WILMINGTON'S LONG MAN

DISTANCE/TIME	6.25 miles (10km) / 2hrs 30min
ASCENT/GRADIENT	465ft (142m) / ▲ ▲
PATHS	Downland paths and tracks, stretch of country road
LANDSCAPE	Dramatic downland on east side of Cuckmere Valley
SUGGESTED MAP	AA Walker's Map 30 Eastbourne & Beachy Head
START/FINISH	Grid reference: TQ543042
DOG FRIENDLINESS	Some enclosed tracks suitable for dogs off lead
PARKING	Free long-stay car park at Wilmington
PUBLIC TOILETS	None on route

One of Britain's most impressive and enduring mysteries is the focal point of this highly scenic walk high on the Downs. Cut into the turf below Windover Hill, the chalk figure of the Long Man of Wilmington is the largest representation of the human figure in Western Europe, and yet it remains an enigma, its origins shrouded in mystery. For centuries experts have been trying to solve this ancient puzzle, but no one has been able to prove conclusively who he is or what he symbolises.

For many years the earliest record of the Long Man was thought to have been a drawing by the antiquarian William Burrell, made when he visited Wilmington Priory in 1766. Then, in 1993, a new drawing was discovered, made by John Rowley, a surveyor, as long ago as 1710. Though the new drawing has confirmed some theories, it has not been able to shed any real light on the Long Man's true identity or why this particular hillside was chosen. However, it does suggest that the original figure was a shadow or indentation in the grass rather than a bold line. It seems there were distinguishing facial features which may have long faded; the staves being held were not a rake and a scythe as once described, and the head was originally a helmet shape, indicating that the Long Man may have been a helmeted war-god.

Until the 19th century the chalk figure was only visible in a certain light, particularly when there was a dusting of snow or frost on the ground. In 1874, a public subscription was raised through *The Times*, and the figure re-cut. To help define the outline of the Long Man, the site was marked out in yellow bricks, though this restoration work may have resulted in the feet being incorrectly positioned.

In 1925 the Long Man of Wilmington was given to the Sussex Archaeological Trust, which later became the Sussex Archaeological Society. During World War II the site was camouflaged to prevent enemy aircraft from using it as a landmark. In 1969 further restoration work began, and the yellow bricks were replaced with pre-cast concrete blocks. These are frequently painted now, so that the shape of the Long Man stands out from a considerable distance away. Photographed from the air, the figure is elongated, but when viewed from ground level an optical illusion is created and he assumes normal human proportions. The walk passes as close as it can to the Long Man before heading out into isolated downland country, where the trees of Friston can be seen cloaking the landscape. Do this walk on a cold winter's day and the Long Man's ghostly aura, and the remoteness of the surroundings, will be enough to send a shiver down the spine.

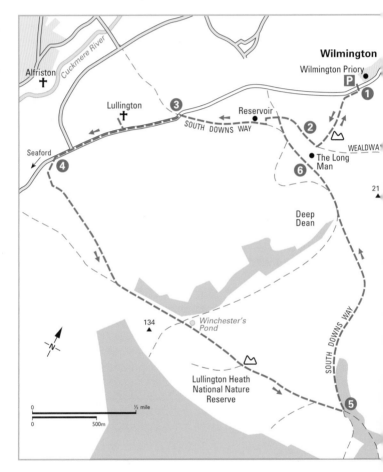

1. Make for the car park exit, cross the road and turn right to follow the path parallel to the road, heading towards the Long Man of Wilmington. Bear left at the barrier and take the Wealdway to the chalk figure. Climb quite steeply, curving to the right. Go through a gate and go straight ahead towards the escarpment, veering right just below the figure of the Long Man.

2. Go through the next gate, cross a track and bear left as soon as a fence-enclosed reservoir comes into view ahead. A few paces brings you to the right of a gate and a sign for the South Downs Way. Turn right on a track and pass the reservoir.

3. Turn left onto the road and walk down to a signpost by two wooden garages for Lullington church, following the path alongside several cottages. After visiting the church, retrace your steps to the road and turn right. Head down the lane and past a turning for Alfriston on the right, and continue ahead towards Seaford.

4. Just after a postbox, turn left on a rising track, signposted 'Jevington'. Follow this as it climbs steadily between tracts of remote downland. Keep left at the next main junction, then at the second junction by a small flint pillar keep forward, past the entrance gate to Winchester's Pond on your left. Lullington Heath National Nature Reserve is on the right now. At the bottom of a dip, continue forward (ignoring a track to the right) and keep on the track as it climbs steeply. Pass a second sign.

5. Where the trees begin, reach a junction with the South Downs Way and turn left to follow the enclosed path to a gate. Go straight ahead slightly above the woodland and pass through a wooden gate. The path begins a gradual curve to the left and eventually passes along the rim of a spectacular dry valley known as Deep Dean. Keep the fence on your left and look for a gate ahead. Swing right as you approach it to a stile and then follow the path to the left of the fence, crossing along the top of the Long Man.

6. Glance to your right and you can just make out the head and body of the chalk figure down below. It's an intriguing view. Continue, keeping the fence on your right, avoiding joining the main track which bends left towards the reservoir, and descend to a gate. Turn right here and retrace your steps to the car park at Wilmington.

Where to eat and drink

At the far end of the car park is a pleasant picnic area. The Giant's Rest in Wilmington is a popular pub at the northern end of the village. Alternatively, by the A27 is the Wishing Well Tea Rooms, serving home-made soups, sandwiches and cakes.

What to see

Wilmington Priory was founded for the Benedictine abbey of Grestain in Normandy, and much of the present building dates from the 14th century. As few as two or three monks resided here, and they used the parish church in Wilmington rather than building their own place of worship. The monks were engaged in managing the abbey's English estates. The priory is in the care of the Landmark Trust and used as a holiday let, so is not open to the public. Only 16ft (5m) square, 13th-century Lullington church stands above the Cuckmere Valley and is one of Britain's smallest churches. (Find more information in the AA's *Tiny Churches* by Dixe Wills.)

While you're there

Make a detour to look at the Lullington Heath National Nature Reserve, which consists of scrubland, chalk grassland and the best example of chalk heath still surviving in Britain. Various heathers and orchids also grow here. Study the maps displayed along the reserve boundary to help you follow the reserve's paths and bridleways.

ARLINGTON'S LAKESIDE TRAIL

DISTANCE/TIME	3 miles (4.8km) / 1hr 30min
ASCENT/GRADIENT	82ft (25m) / ▲
PATHS	Field paths and trails, some brief road walking, many stiles
LANDSCAPE	Level lakeside terrain and gentle farmland
SUGGESTED MAP	AA Walker's Map 30 Eastbourne & Beachy Head
START/FINISH	Grid reference: TQ528074
DOG FRIENDLINESS	Mostly on lead, as requested by signs on route
PARKING	Fee-paying car park at Arlington Reservoir
PUBLIC TOILETS	At car park

In 1971 Arlington's landscape changed irrevocably when a vital new reservoir was opened, supplying water to Eastbourne, Hailsham, Polegate and Heathfield. The 120-acre (46ha) reservoir was formed by cleverly cutting off a meander in the Cuckmere River, and it's now an established site for wintering wildfowl, as well as home to a successful trout fishery. Besides the trout, bream, perch, roach and eels make up Arlington's underwater population. The lake draws anglers from all over Sussex.

The local nature reserve was originally planted with more than 30,000 native trees, including oak, birch, wild cherry, hazel and hawthorn. The grassland areas along the shoreline are intentionally left uncut to enable many kinds of moth and butterfly to thrive in their natural habitats. Orchids grow here too. The reservoir is a designated Site of Special Scientific Interest (SSSI), and a favourite haunt of many birds on spring and autumn migrations; up to 10,000 wildfowl spend their winters here, including large numbers of mallard and wigeon. The shoveller duck is also a frequent visitor, and most common as a bird of passage. You can identify the head of the drake by its dark, bottle-green colouring and broad bill. The breast is white and the underparts bright chestnut, while its brown and black back has a noticeable blue sheen. The female duck is mottled brown.

Great crested grebes, Canada geese and nightingales are also known to inhabit the reservoir area, making Arlington a popular destination for ornithologists. See if you can spot the blue flash of a kingfisher on the water; its colouring so distinctive it would be hard to confuse it with any other bird. It's also known for its piercing whistles as it swoops low over the water. The reservoir and its environs are home to fallow deer and foxes, so keep a sharp look-out as you walk around the lake.

The walk begins in the main car park by the reservoir, though initially views of the lake are obscured by undergrowth and a curtain of trees. After visiting the village of Arlington, where there is a welcome pub, the return leg is directly beside the water, providing a constantly changing scenic backdrop to round off the walk.

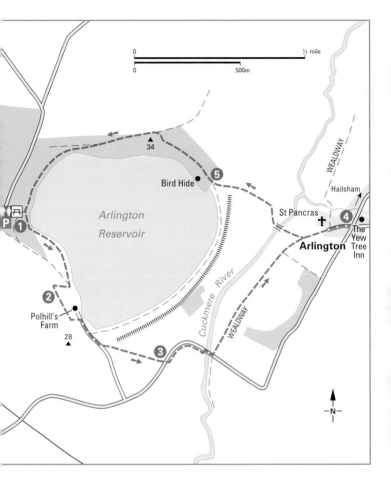

1. From the car park walk towards the information board and map. Pass this and turn right on the circular walk by the reservoir, soon passing a small picnic area, and ignoring a fork to the right. Carry on until eventually the path reaches a driveway, with a gate to the left signed 'No entry farm access only'; here cross over, following the footpath and bridleway signs.

2. Skirt the buildings of Polhill's Farm and return to the tarmac lane. Turn right and walk along to a kissing gate on your left and a 'circular walk' sign. Ignore the gate and keep on the lane. Continue for about 50yds (46m) and then branch left over a stile into a field. Swing half right and look for two stiles tucked away in a fence corner. Ignore the first one you come to and cross the second, passing an overgrown pond to your left. Cross a third stile and go across a pasture to a fourth stile.

3. Cross the road and turn left to follow the path parallel with the road. Rejoin the road, cross the Cuckmere River and then bear left to join the Wealdway, following the sign for Arlington. Walk along the drive and when it curves to the right, by some houses, veer left over a stile. Head for the spire of Arlington church, keeping ahead when you reach the right-hand fence corner and

following the waymark. Cross another stile and a wooden footbridge. Keep to the right of the church, cross another stile and walk along the lane to the Yew Tree Inn.

4. From the pub, retrace your steps to the church and cross over the field to the footbridge. Turn right immediately beyond it to a stile in the field corner. Cross the pasture to the prominent metal footbridge over the Cuckmere and continue to cross over a plank bridge, then head across the field towards a line of trees, following the vague outline of a path. The reservoir's embankment is clearly defined on the left as you begin a gentle ascent.

5. Cross a stile by a galvanised gate and go through a kissing gate on the immediate right. Follow the path alongside the lake and pass a bird hide on the left. Keep left further on and keep to the bridleway, as it reveals glimpses of the lake through the trees. Veer left at the fork and then follow the path alongside the reservoir back to the car park.

Where to eat and drink

Arlington Reservoir has both a picnic site and a small open-air café by the car park where you can relax before or after the walk. The Yew Tree Inn at Arlington has a children's play area, a beer garden and a choice of home-cooked dishes. Lunch and dinner are served every day and there is a choice of real ales. Nearby are the Arlington Tea Rooms and the Old Oak Inn, originally the village almshouse and dating from the 17th century.

What to see

Call into Arlington's St Pancras Church. It has Saxon origins, as seen in its 'long and short work' outside, and fragments of wall paintings inside, as well as an impressive timber roof with huge kingposts and trusses.

While you're there

Stop off at the Arlington bird hide and see if you can identify members of Arlington's feathered population. In spring you might spot an osprey, a large bird which occasionally visits lakes, fens and estuaries and preys almost exclusively on fish. Look out too for house martins, sand martins, sandpipers, blackcaps, kestrels, mallards and dunlins, among other birds.

ALFRISTON AND BERWICK

DISTANCE/TIME	4 miles (6.4km) / 2hrs
ASCENT/GRADIENT	464ft (141m) / ▲ ▲
PATHS	Exposed paths and tracks
LANDSCAPE	Downland to west of Cuckmere Valley
SUGGESTED MAP	AA Walker's Map 30 Eastbourne & Beachy Head
START/FINISH	Grid reference: TQ520033
DOG FRIENDLINESS	Mostly off lead but not permitted at Alfriston Clergy House
PARKING	The Willows fee-paying car park, Alfriston; free parking in the smaller car park in the centre of the village (maximum 3hrs)
PUBLIC TOILETS	Alfriston

With its charming shops, inns and church, Alfriston is a classic Sussex village. Situated at the foot of the South Downs in a gap fashioned by the Cuckmere River, it's the perfect place to explore on foot.

St Andrew's Church, known as the 'Cathedral of the Downs', occupies a secluded setting by a spacious green, hidden away from the main street. Standing on an ancient Anglo Saxon mound, it is said to mark the spot where four oxen, carrying building materials, lay down to rest. It has a large musicians' gallery, unusually installed as recently as 1995 to provide extra space. At the centre of the village are the weathered remains of the market cross. It is one of only two such structures in Sussex (the other being in Chichester) and is thought to date from 1405, when Henry IV granted the village the right to hold a market. A lorry collided with it in 1955, and the shaft is a modern replacement; on top is a carving of a shepherd's crown, a good-luck charm traditionally carried by shepherds.

In centuries past, Alfriston was rife with smuggling activities and harboured one of the most notorious smugglers' gangs. The Market Cross Inn, also known as Ye Olde Smugglers Inne, was once home to gang-leader Stanton Collins, and reputedly contained numerous secret staircases and hiding holes.

From the outside, Berwick's church looks like any other country church, but once inside look for the time switch and light up the interior. That way you can appreciate the remarkable wall paintings in all their detail. These murals were commissioned by Bishop Bell of Chichester in 1943 and are the work of Duncan Grant and Vanessa and Quentin Bell, members of the renowned Bloomsbury Group, who lived nearby at Charleston. During World War II many church windows were destroyed by bombs, and the Bishop of Chichester considered it more appropriate for artists to decorate church walls rather than design windows. Familiar landmarks were used in the paintings, and local people took part as models. In one scene, over the chancel arch, a soldier and airman from Firle and a sailor from Berwick are seen kneeling.

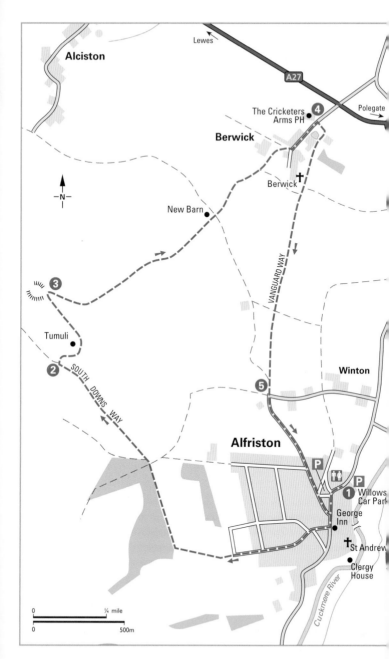

1. Turn left on leaving the car park, by the tourism leaflets dispenser, and make for the centre of Alfriston. Pass the cross in the main street and turn right by the Star Inn, following Star Lane. Go straight over at the junction up King's Ride and continue on the South Downs Way. The road dwindles to a steep flinty track further up. This was originally a drovers' route for sheep

being driven to market. Pass two tracks on the right and follow the wide track as it curves gently to the right. Continue on the South Downs Way, forking right at a signpost, then just after cross a track to take a gate ahead. Proceed along a fence and keep going over this high ground. This stretch of the walk gives exhilarating views over the Downs and towards Alfriston.

2. Turn right through the next gate, signposted 'Public Bridleway', initially following the path between fences, then bending to the left and dropping steeply. The smooth expanse of Arlington Reservoir is visible in the distance.

3. 75yds (68m) beyond a gate halfway down the slope, turn sharp right at a junction. Follow the clear path towards the distant spire of Berwick church, joining a hedgerow, and soon forking right at a signpost. Continue along a narrow woodland strip between fields. Join a track near a huge converted barn, turn right on it, then immediately swing left. Pass a bridleway on the right and continue on the track. Swing right at an ivy-clad corrugated barn populated by swallows in the summer, and walk along to The Cricketers Arms.

4. Join the unwaymarked shingle track opposite the pub, first crossing an area often used for parking. Veer right around the pond, pass between houses to reach a nettle-strewn path and then a stile with a Vanguard Way sign. Cross a field to the gate to Berwick church. Enter the churchyard to view the church. Leave by the same gate, returning to the Vanguard Way by turning right along the field edge, and right again to a gate in the corner. Go straight on at the junction at a point level with the end of the churchyard, following VGW markers. Descend to a gate and follow the waymarked path across open fields, keep forward at the next junction, then climb to join a gravel drive.

5. Go straight ahead at a road, avoiding Winton Street on the left. Descend the slope into Alfriston and bear left for the car park, or continue into the village.

Where to eat and drink
The Star at Alfriston has log fires in winter, and serves morning coffee and bar meals. The timbered 14th-century George Inn on the High Street is a cosy place to stop, and has a secluded garden, while the Market Cross (also known as the Smugglers) is a traditional village local. The Singing Kettle, Chestnuts and Badgers Tea House serve morning coffee, light lunches and afternoon tea and are located in the village centre. The Cricketers Arms at Berwick serves traditional home-made food, with the emphasis on local produce, meat and fish, and locally brewed cask ales.

What to see
On the edge of the green at Alfriston is an old mine, washed up on the Cuckmere River in October 1943 and rendered inactive by the naval authorities in World War II.

While you're there
Visit the National Trust's Clergy House at Alfriston. This dates back to about 1350 and was built to cater for a number of confined parish priests in the aftermath of the Black Death. The National Trust acquired the Clergy House as its very first property in 1896, paying just £10 for it.

THE SNAKE RIVER AND CUCKMERE HAVEN

DISTANCE/TIME	5.25 miles (8.5km) / 2hr 30min
ASCENT/GRADIENT	590ft (180m) / ▲ ▲
PATHS	Grassy trails and well-used paths, mostly beside the Cuckmere or the canalised branch of the river, as well as thick woodland; several stiles
LANDSCAPE	Exposed and isolated valley and river mouth
SUGGESTED MAP	AA Walker's Map 30 Eastbourne & Beachy Head
START/FINISH	Grid reference: TV518995
DOG FRIENDLINESS	Under close control within Seven Sisters Country Park. On lead during lambing season, near roads and in Friston Forest
PARKING	Fee-paying car park at Seven Sisters Country Park
PUBLIC TOILETS	Opposite car park, by visitor centre

One of the few remaining undeveloped river mouths in the southeast is the gap or cove known as Cuckmere Haven. It is one of the south coast's best-known and most popular beauty spots. The Cuckmere River joins the English Channel here, but not before it makes a series of extraordinarily wide loops through lush water-meadows, hence the name 'Snake River'. The Cuckmere emerges beside the famous white chalk cliffs known as the Seven Sisters. Extending east towards Birling Gap, there are, in fact, eight of these towering chalk faces, with the highest one, Haven Brow (253ft/77m), closest to the river mouth.

The focal point of the lower valley is the Seven Sisters Country Park. There are artificial lakes and park trails, and a visitor centre. However, there is more to the park than just these attractions. The flowers and insects found here are at their best in early to mid summer, while spring and autumn are a good time to bring your binoculars with you for a close-up view of migrant birds. Early migrant wheatears are sometimes spotted in the vicinity of the river mouth from late February onwards and are followed later in the season by martins, swallows, whinchats and warblers. Keep a careful eye out for whitethroats, terns and waders too. The lakes and lagoons tend to attract waders such as curlews, sandpipers and little stints. Grey phalaropes have also been seen in the park, usually after severe autumn storms.

The walk explores this very special part of the Cuckmere Valley and begins by heading for the beach. The meltwaters of the last Ice Age shaped this landscape, and over the centuries rising sea levels and a freshwater peat swamp influenced the river's route. Around the start of the 19th century, the sea rose to today's level and a new straight cut with raised banks, devised in 1846, shortened the Cuckmere's journey. This helps prevent flooding, although in the long term the plan is to allow the valley to revert to salt marsh.

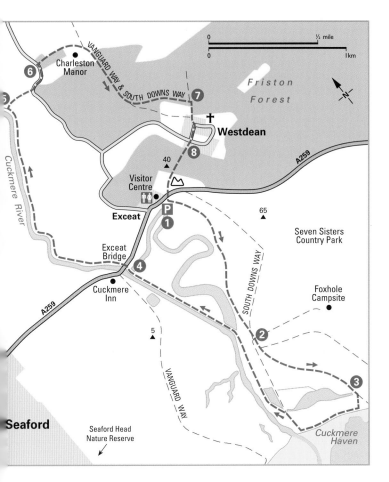

1. From the car park, go through the gate by the parking ticket machine and Seven Sisters Country Park notice board and map, and follow the wide, grassy path signed 'Beach Trail'. The path gradually curves to the right, running parallel to a concrete track. The Cuckmere River meanders beside you, heading for the sea. Continue ahead and make for a South Downs Way sign.

2. Reach a junction with the South Downs Way, avoiding the track to the left over a cattlegrid signposted to Foxhole Campsite. Carry on along through a gate, forking left on the South Downs Way at the next signpost. At the following gate do not follow the South Downs Way uphill but keep right along low ground with the hillside and fence on your left. Pass a group of wartime pill boxes, and go through a gate. Join a stony path and walk ahead to the beach, with the white wall of the Seven Sisters rearing up beside you.

3. Turn right and cross the shore via the shingle beach. Turn right when you reach the river and drop to an Emergency Point sign. Go ahead for about 50yds (46m) until you come to a junction by a line of toothlike concrete wartime tank traps and keep left, following the Park Trail. Keep beside the Cuckmere. The

landscape here is characterised by a network of meandering channels and waterways, all feeding into the river. Keep left at the next fork and follow the footpath as it veers left, in line with the Cuckmere. Continue on the straight path by the side of the river.

4. Cross the road beside Exceat Bridge. Turn left then immediately right through a kissing gate to continue with the Cuckmere on your left, following the riverside path through this delightful, though lonely, valley. Swans may be seen gliding on the water. Head for a kissing gate, continue over two stiles and look for a path on the right, just before a stile.

5. Take the path away from the Cuckmere, following it between trees and bushes. Go through a kissing gate then cross a stile, turn left at the road and pass the entrance to Charleston Manor. Pevsner described Charleston as 'a perfect house in a perfect setting'. Parts of it date from the early 12th century, and the house is renowned for its truly splendid gardens and 15th-century double tithe barn.

6. Continue for a few paces and turn right to join an unwaymarked path, with a wooden fence to your right. Merge with the South Downs Way and the Vanguard Way and keep right at the fork. Climb the steps and follow the signs for the South Downs Way first south, then southeast through Friston Forest. Cut through beech woodland to an obvious junction.

7. Turn right here and drop straight down to the picturesque hamlet of Westdean, lying half-hidden in a wooded hollow. The church dates mostly from the 14th century, and rectory is probably Norman. Join the road on a bend and continue ahead to a junction. Cross over and walk ahead to a flight of steps.

8. Make for a stone stile at the top of the steps, where there are glorious views of the Cuckmere River below winding away towards the sea. This certainly has to be one of the most dramatic and memorable views in all of Sussex. Descend the steep, grassy hillside and make for a kissing gate by the visitor centre. Cross the road and return to the car park.

Where to eat and drink

The Cuckmere Inn by Exceat Bridge is a popular 18th-century inn thought to have inspired Rudyard Kipling's poem 'Song of the Smugglers'. By the visitor centre at the Seven Sisters Country Park is the Saltmarsh, and in summer there is often an ice cream van in the car park.

What to see

Shingle plants thrive on the sheltered parts of beaches; a stroll at Cuckmere Haven reveals the yellow horned poppy and the fleshy leaved sea kale. Sea beet, curled dock and scentless chamomile also grow here. On the west side of the valley is a huge carving of a horse known as Litlington White Horse.

While you're there

If you have the time, take a look at the Seaford Head Nature Reserve. This chalk headland, which rises 282ft (85m) above the sea, is a popular local attraction and from here the coastal views are magnificent.

FIRLE TOWER AND BEYOND

DISTANCE/TIME	4.75 miles (7.6km) / 2hr 30mins
ASCENT/GRADIENT	476ft (145m) / ▲ ▲
PATHS	Grassy tracks, village street and field paths; no stiles
LANDSCAPE	Downland and farmland
SUGGESTED MAP	AA Walker's Map 30 Eastbourne & Beachy Head
START/FINISH	Grid reference: TQ468075
DOG FRIENDLINESS	On lead in vicinity of Firle Place and where livestock is grazing
PARKING	Free car park in Firle village
PUBLIC TOILETS	There are toilets at Charleston – these were even open when the house was closed, and there doesn't seem anything to stop walkers using them

Firle is a perfect example of what landscape historians describe as a 'closed village'. Such settlements, growing up on private estates, enjoy a unique status and are a vivid reminder of the autocracy of generations of powerful land-owning families. The development of Firle was severely regulated, and it was virtually impossible for outsiders to move into the village, which has for many years provided important employment and accommodation opportunities, operating as a self-contained community.

Arts events

Touching on the ever-popular South Downs Way and taking in a patchwork of fields and glorious vistas, this bracing walk takes you up and away from Firle's quaint old village streets, past Firle Beacon and on to Charleston Farmhouse, once home to artists Vanessa Bell and Duncan Grant. This unique museum preserves and promotes the legacy of the Bloomsbury Group – a loose collective of influential English writers, intellectuals, philosophers and artists working in the first half of the 20th century, including Virginia Woolf, John Maynard Keynes, E M Forster and Lytton Strachey. The house and garden are full of rich colours, wonderful artworks and inspiring ideas. The programme of events includes art classes for all the family, and there is an annual festival in May, an ideal month in which to do this walk.

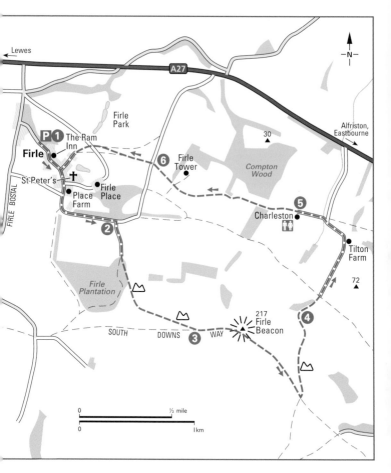

1. Turn left out of the car park, pass The Ram Inn and follow the road round to the right, through the village of Firle. Walk past the village stores (ignore the turning to the left) and head out of the village. Past the last building keep straight on, avoiding turning to right. The track curves left, with the estate wall on the left.

2. Just beyond the end of the first field on the right, turn right at a waymarker post, on a track up the right side of the field, along the strip of woodland. At the top of the field, go through a gate and carry on up the grassy spur ahead.

3. At the top of the ridge, turn left along the South Downs Way, with views of the coast to the south. Carry on through a gate – there are tumuli (burial mounds) on either side of it – to your right, and pass the trig point. The path then drops, and soon after it levels out and rises very gently, turn sharp left at a waymarker post by a couple of gorse bushes, leaving the South Downs Way. The path soon becomes pronounced, and drops through a gate.

4. At the foot of the main slope, continue through the waymarked gate half right, down alongside woodland before continuing forward at a junction of

tracks. Pass a house called Tilton Meadow and turn left at the next junction, by some barns. Follow the concrete bridleway past a right-angled bend, then immediately after turn left towards Charleston.

5. Past Charleston, go through a gate and continue ahead on a track, then forward along the left edge of a field. Go through the gate on the left at the far corner, then turn right to resume the same direction, up across fields and just below Firle Tower. This Gothic eye-catcher was built in 1819 to accommodate the estate gamekeeper. Cross a track, pass through trees and enter a field. Firle Place, in its lovely downland setting, can be seen from here. Keep to the right-hand edge of the field, and almost immediately bear diagonally left towards some houses. Join a wall and go through the gap at the wall corner. Go through a wrought-iron gate between houses.

6. Cross the lane to a gate and follow the marker posts through the parkland of Firle Place. Eventually merge into a track joining from the right, and cross the main estate road. Follow the track ahead, to take a gate to the left of the cricket ground, and follow this to the road. Turn right on Firle's village street to return to the car park.

Where to eat and drink

There is a fabulous café housed in Charleston's charming historic outbuildings. Open whenever the house and garden are open, the café serves wholesome lunches or afternoon teas, and welcomes ramblers. Seasonal ingredients and locally sourced produce are used wherever possible.

What to see

Firle Escarpment is a Site of Special Scientific Interest (SSSI). The large area of chalkland is home to a variety of flora and fauna. Look out for the rare spider orchid *Ophrys sphegodes*.

While you're there

Keep a look-out for Peter Owen Jones, Firle's 'celebrity' vicar. Well known for his thought-provoking television documentaries on spirituality and exploring the British countryside, he is author of the fascinating walking book *Everest England* from AA Publishing.

DOWNLAND VIEWS OVER FIRLE

DISTANCE/TIME	3.75 miles (6km) / 2hrs
ASCENT/GRADIENT	689ft (201m) / ▲ ▲
PATHS	Tracks, paths and roads
LANDSCAPE	Downland and farmland
SUGGESTED MAP	AA Walker's Map 30 Eastbourne & Beachy Head
START/FINISH	Grid reference: TQ468075
DOG FRIENDLINESS	On lead in vicinity of Firle Place and near livestock
PARKING	Free car park in Firle
PUBLIC TOILETS	Firle Place (visitors only)

Stroll along the South Downs Way between Alfriston and the River Ouse and you can look down towards the sleepy village of Firle, nestling amid a patchwork of fields and hedgerows below the escarpment. There is something that sets this place apart from most other communities. Firle is an estate village with a tangible feudal atmosphere.

At the centre of the village lies Firle Place, home to the Gage family for over 500 years and now open to the public. The 18th-century house is magnificent, though it hardly looks classically English. It's built of a pale stone specially imported from Caen in Normandy, with hipped roof, dormers and a splendid Venetian window surmounting the rusticated central archway in the east front. Firle Place is surrounded by glorious parkland and set against a magnificent backdrop of hanging woods. The name is Old English and means 'oak'. No house could occupy a finer location. A tour of the house reveals some fascinating treasures, many of which were brought back from America by Sir Thomas Gage. The paintings include an important collection of Old Masters with works by Van Dyck, Reynolds, Gainsborough and Rubens, and there are also collections of Sèvres porcelain and English and French furniture.

The present Palladian mansion conceals part of an older Tudor building. This was later enlarged by Sir John Gage, Vice Chamberlain and Captain of the Royal Guard in the court of Henry VIII. In 1542, when James V of Scotland was killed at Solway Moss, he commanded the King's troops against the Scottish army. He also superintended the executions of Queen Catherine Howard and Lady Jane Grey, while Constable of the Tower of London. Sir Edward Gage, his son, as Sheriff of Sussex, was responsible for ensuring that the Lewes Martyrs were burned, but the family later converted to the Roman Catholic faith and were forced to retire from public life. Little remains of the external features of the original courtyard house. The house underwent major changes in 1745, remodelled by General Sir Thomas Gage, who was Commander-in-Chief of the British forces at the beginning of the American War of Independence. He and his cousin and successor, Sir Thomas, rebuilt the house in the Palladian style with many elaborate rococo features.

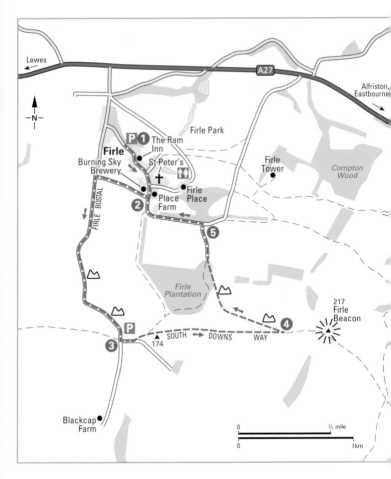

1. Turn left out of the car park, pass The Ram Inn and then follow the road round to the right, through the village of Firle. Walk along to the village stores and a footpath to Charleston. Pass the turning to Firle's Church of St Peter and continue heading southwards, out of the village, passing the Burning Sky brewery in Place Barn to your right.

2. Turn right at a junction of concrete tracks and make for the road. Bear left, head for the downland escarpment and begin the long climb, steep in places. On reaching the car park at the top, swing left to a gate and join the South Downs Way.

3. Head eastwards on the long-distance trail, passing a square concrete tank.

4. When you reach a blue-arrowed marker post about 200yds (183m) before a very noticeable gate at a high point on the ridge, turn sharp left, initially along the top but soon heading down the steep slopes of the escarpment. Keep descending all the way, as the path veers right. Drop down to reach a gate and walk ahead, keeping a fence on your left. Skirt around Firle Plantation and follow the track all the way to the junction, ignoring a track passing through a double gate to your left.

5. Bear left and walk along the track, alongside the estate wall on your right, keeping the dramatic escarpment on your left. As you approach the village of Firle, the track curves to the right towards the buildings of Place Farm. Cross over the junction of concrete tracks and retrace your steps back to the car park at the other end of the village.

Where to eat and drink

The Ram Inn at Firle serves imaginative food all day from 9am to 9.30pm and is a fine example of a traditional, old-style village pub. Firle Place has a licensed tea room serving tea, coffee and cakes. There is a tea terrace offering delightful views over the gardens.

What to see

Firle's Burning Sky Brewery occupies re-purposed farm buildings in the village. The brewery's first beer was produced in 2013 and by the following year it had already been named the 4th Best New Brewery in the World by the Ratebeer website. It's also Britain's first craft brewery to use oak foudres for the ageing process.

While you're there

It's always pleasing to find a church open to visitors, and many in Sussex keep their doors unlocked throughout the year. Firle church is no exception, and the sign at the entrance states that the door is open from dawn to dusk. The parish refuses 'to be deterred by occasional thefts, believing it must be available to the people of the village'. There is a fee for brass rubbing, which should be paid at the village stores. The church includes a window dedicated to Henry Rainald Gage KCVO, the 6th Viscount, who succeeded to the title in his 17th year in 1912 and died in 1982. The window depicting a ram and the South Downs was designed by the late John Piper, and is possibly his last work in stained glass.

AROUND ASHDOWN FOREST

DISTANCE/TIME	7 miles (11.3km) / 3hrs 30min
ASCENT/GRADIENT	170ft (52m) / ▲
PATHS	Paths and tracks across farmland and woodland, many stiles
LANDSCAPE	Undulating farmland and dense woodland
SUGGESTED MAP	OS Explorer 135 Ashdown Forest
START/FINISH	Grid reference: TQ471332
DOG FRIENDLINESS	Some woodland stretches suitable for dogs off lead. On lead where notices indicate
PARKING	Pooh car park (free), off B2026 south of Hartfield
PUBLIC TOILETS	None on route
NOTES	Five Hundred Acre Wood is privately owned; keep to the Wealdway

If as a child you were spellbound by Winnie-the-Pooh, then this enjoyable woodland walk will rekindle memories of A A Milne's wonderful stories. The walk skirts Ashdown Forest, the real-life setting for Winnie-the-Pooh, and the largest area of uncultivated land in southeast England, covering about 20 square miles (58sq km). The area is an attractive mix of high, open heathland and oak and birch woodland scattered across the well-wooded sandstone hills of the High Weald. William Cobbett described it as 'verily the most villainously ugly spot I ever saw in England', though exploring the forest today, it would be hard to agree with him.

Ashdown was a royal forest for 300 years, established by John of Gaunt in 1372. Then, it was a place of wild beauty and thick woodland. After the Restoration of Charles II in 1660, large parts of the forest were enclosed and given to Royalist supporters. About 6,400 acres (2,600ha) were dedicated to the Commoners, and remain freely accessible to the public. Ashdown Forest is cared for by Conservators, and today is the domain of the city-dweller seeking peaceful recreation in the country. Despite this, it is still largely unspoilt.

At first glance, the forest's vegetation may look uniform, but closer inspection reveals greater variety. In the valley bottoms, wet bogs are dominated by sphagnum mosses. Round-leaved sundew, marsh clubmoss and cottongrass also thrive. The deep blue flowers of marsh gentians add a dash of colour during the autumn. The open pools are home to the nymphs of dragonflies and damselflies, while the drier valley slopes are carpeted with plants such as ling, bell heather and bracken. The higher ground supports gorse and purple moor-grass.

The walk begins in a corner of (privately owned) Five Hundred Acre Wood. The return leg briefly follows a disused railway line before heading south across rolling countryside, passing close to Cotchford Farm, where Milne lived, and crossing Pooh Bridge, built in 1907 and restored in 1979.

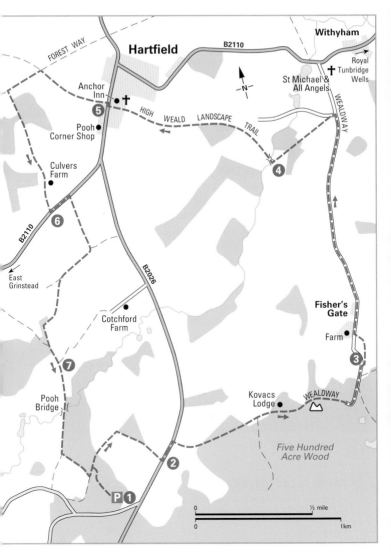

1. Follow the path through the gate at the bottom of the car park, signposted 'P. Bridge', and just after a path joins from the left, fork right over a plank bridge and over a stile to enter a field. Go forward along the left-hand field-edge to a track in the corner; turn right. Cross a drive to a gap in the hedge and keep ahead, ignoring a hedge-side way marked 'Alternative Path'. Follow the path through two gates and across a paddock to a stile and the road.

2. Turn left onto the road, then bear right opposite The Paddocks and through Five Hundred Acre Wood, taking a left fork and crossing a stream by a foot-bridge to reach the Wealdway. Continue ahead, following WW markers, passing Kovacs Lodge. Follow further WW markers along a lane, keeping left at a junction, then just after Honeywood House bear left to leave the forest and take the path to the right of two gates, below the sign for 'Fisher's Gate'.

3. Follow the path parallel to the drive to skirt the house. Rejoin the drive and keep right, following the Wealdway as it cuts across undulating farmland for 0.75 miles (1.2km). Pass a turning to Old Buckhurst and then bear left over a stile hidden in bracken, just before a driveway to Forstal Cottage, to follow the High Weald Landscape Trail. Cross the field past a clump of trees to enter woodland. Follow the woodland track, soon forking right.

4. Turn right over a brick bridge at the far side of the wood and bear right to follow the fence, passing a house. Go through the gateway in the field corner and make for the next field ahead. Head diagonally left across farmland to a stile. Keep to the right edge of the field to a stile, then cross a footbridge and continue by the field-edge towards the church. Turn left at a stile and enter the village of Hartfield.

5. Bear right at the B2026, then immediately left along the left-hand edge of a recreation ground, the home of Hartfield FC. Keep the tennis courts on your right to cross a stile in the field corner and continue over the next stile and onto the Forest Way. Turn left and follow the old railway trackbed, forking left to a gate just before the trackbed crosses a bridge. Cross the pasture to a gate and follow the woodland bridleway. Emerging from the trees, continue to Culvers Farm.

6. Turn left on the road and walk along to the first right-hand footpath, signposted 'Pooh Bridge'. Take the track ahead, soon passing a wooden shelter and, after going through woodland, emerge by fields and turn right on an enclosed path past a white house. Cross a drive to another stile and head diagonally down the field to a stile in the corner, passing through a kissing gate on the way. Continue on the path and head for the kissing gate, then follow the lane ahead and slightly to the left.

7. After 80yds (73m), fork right by a signpost, go straight on along the public bridleway to Pooh Bridge, and follow the track all the way to Pooh car park, avoiding minor side turnings.

Where to eat and drink

There is a popular tea room in the Pooh Corner Shop, and, on the route of the walk, in the village centre is the Anchor Inn, which serves food.

What to see

Approaching the village of Hartfield, note the 700-year-old church and its ancient lych gate, which includes a good example of pargeting or ornamental plasterwork. Picturesque Lych Gate Cottage is one of the oldest and smallest houses in the area. Try to find the plaque indicating an approximate date of 1520 and go into the churchyard for a better view of this lovely old building. Nearby is an ancient yew tree, often found in country churchyards. The yew is thought to be a symbol of mortality and resurrection, providing protection from evil.

FOREST ROW AND ASHDOWN FOREST

DISTANCE/TIME	5.5 miles (8.8km) / 1hr 15min
ASCENT/GRADIENT	50ft (15m) / ▲
PATHS	Pavements in Forest Row, a former railway trackbed, lanes and field paths, several stiles
LANDSCAPE	Rolling countryside and the headwaters of the River Medway
SUGGESTED MAP	OS Explorer 135 Ashdown Forest
START/FINISH	Grid reference: TQ426349
DOG FRIENDLINESS	On lead in Forest Row and in livestock fields around Burnthouse Farm
PARKING	Car park on Hartfield Road
PUBLIC TOILETS	None on route

If ever a name sounded like a Victorian suburban confection, Forest Row is it, but in fact it is an old settlement and was a highly descriptive name. Most small settlements that grew up on the edge of Ashdown Forest were clumps of sporadic cottages straggling into shapeless hamlets. Forest Row, unusually, was developed as a single street of houses, or 'row', and is first mentioned by name in 1467 as 'Forstrowe', and then in 1546 as 'Forest Rowe'.

By the mid-19th century Forest Row was a hamlet with a few houses around a square green that has been partly built over by the 1836 parish church. Built as a chapel of ease within the then parish of East Grinstead, Forest Row did not become a fully independent parish until 1894. This was probably in recognition of the village's expansion after the East Grinstead and Tunbridge Wells Railway station opened in 1866.

The most flamboyant building in the village is Freshfield Hall, which faces south behind a small triangular green with a fine war memorial. Built for Henry Freshfield of nearby Kidbrooke Park in 1892, it is in local Sussex style, with ornate plasterwork in the gable and around the tablet dedicated to Freshfield's son, who had died in 1891. The architect was a Scot, John M Brydon, who pulled out all the stops for his patron.

After leaving the railway trackbed the walk passes the romantic ruins of Brambletye House. Three three-storey towers survive, with bits of the linking walls. The central entrance tower has the date '1631' in a lozenge, and the southern tower retains its leaded ogee roof. This is the front elevation of the house, the sides and rear having long been demolished. It was built in the finest cut local sandstone and had large mullioned windows. The ruins are set back from the lane, fronted by the remains of the gatehouse and courtyard walls. The house was built for Sir Henry Compton, who died around 1649. He was a lawyer who, through his connections with the powerful Sackvilles of East Grinstead, was appointed a ranger of Ashdown Forest, a Justice of the Peace and MP for East Grinstead. However, it seems that Brambletye was abandoned by the end of the 17th century. There is another site nearby, its moat largely intact, and it is thought that this was the location of an earlier manor house. This was listed in the Domesday Book of 1086 as 'Branbertei', and in 1091 as 'Brembeltie' – an enclosure where brambles grow.

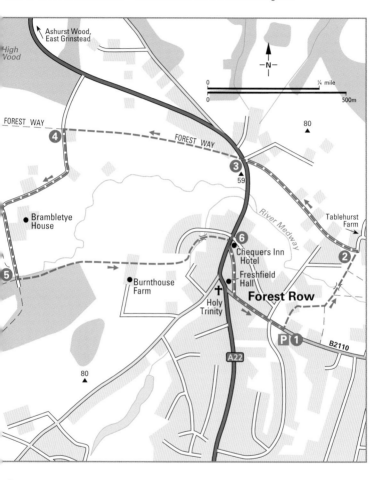

1. From the car park cross Hartfield Road via the pedestrian crossing. Continue to the left of the shops onto a private driveway that very soon leads to a path, Forester's Link. Follow this round to the right and go to the right of the exercise park. The track skirts a timber yard, turns left at a waymarked T-junction and crosses a stream, the upper reaches of the River Medway, on a footbridge. Continue to a signboard for the Forest Way Country Park.

2. At the signboard go left and follow the footpath, signed 'National Cycle Network 21'. Ascend to the right of a scout hut, then bear left onto a lane which passes a veterinary surgery and follow it to the main road, the A22.

3. Cross the road via the pedestrian crossing lights and go up a tarmac path to join the railway trackbed, now a multi-user path, and part of the Forest Way waymarked route.

4. At Brambletye Crossing leave the trackbed path and go left onto a lane. The lane bears right and passes the fascinating ruins of Brambletye House. Continue past the ruin, and with the 17th-century stone boundary wall on your left. Pass the gates to Brambletye Manor Farmhouse and go left onto a track. To your right, lumps in the grassy field mark the site of Brambletye House's predecessor. Cross a stone bridge over the Medway, whose upper reaches were dammed in the 1950s to form Weir Wood Reservoir 0.5 miles (800m) to your right.

5. Immediately after the bridge, at the footpath crossroads, go left through a kissing gate. Continue with a young ash and oak wood on your right, cross a stile into a field and bear half right, leaving the river bank, towards a timber-framed farmhouse, Burnthouse Farm. Over a stile ascend towards the house and barn. At the barn, go left and over a stile and turn right to another two stiles. After the second stile, bear left to continue alongside the left-hand hedge in pasture. Cross a stile and continue within scrub, the path meandering through to a footbridge. Cross this, winding along a shingle path beside the stream to emerge in the car park of a block of flats. Go up two flights of steps to pass beneath the flats and shops to Lewes Road, back in Forest Row.

6. Bear right towards the spiky spire of the parish church of the Holy Trinity, a modest stone building of 1836. Beyond the tile-hung and timber-framed Chequers Inn Hotel cross the road at the pedestrian lights and continue ahead behind the village hall to bear right along the quieter road with shops, and then turn left down Hartfield Road to return to the car park.

Where to eat and drink

Pubs and restaurants in and around Forest Row include the Chequers Inn Hotel in a 15th-century timber-framed house, which serves good bar-snack meals. The organic Tablehurst Farm has an excellent café with garden open Monday to Saturday. It serves freshly made pies, pastries, salads and cakes, including vegan and gluten-free options.

What to see

Part of this walk follows the trackbed of the former East Grinstead to Tunbridge Wells Railway that opened in 1866. Closed from East Grinstead to Groombridge in 1967, much of it is now the Forest Way path for cyclists and walkers. The eastern section of the line to Tunbridge Wells was opened in 1996 as the heritage steam Spa Valley Railway.

While you're there

To the motorist, East Grinstead is a bypass and a traffic delay, but in fact it has a superb historic core with a 13th-century marketplace and a High Street lined with medieval and Tudor timber-framed buildings. At the east end is Sackville College, a quadrangle of mellow sandstone buildings founded as almshouses in 1617 by the Earl of Dorset.

BARCOMBE MILLS

DISTANCE/TIME	2.75 miles (4.4km) / 1hr 30min
ASCENT/GRADIENT	Negligible
PATHS	Riverside paths, a former railway line trackbed
LANDSCAPE	River banks and the course of a dismantled railway
SUGGESTED MAPS	OS Explorer OL11 Brighton & Hove
START/FINISH	Grid reference: TQ434146
DOG FRIENDLINESS	On lead in livestock fields
PARKING	Public car park on Barcombe Mills Road, off the A26
PUBLIC TOILETS	None on route

Apart from the hamlet's name, the many bridges and the complex water courses at the start of the walk – fast-flowing over weirs or directed powerfully through sluices – give a clue to the fact that there were once very large watermills here. Some channels are millstreams, and some are millraces. The oil mills and button factory buildings burned down in 1939, leaving only their diverted and controlled watercourses. This was where the Ouse ceased being a tidal river, but the area is still prone to flooding.

It is thought there were watermills here as early as Roman times, but the first recorded examples are in the Domesday Book, that great land-ownership and tax register compiled on William the Conqueror's orders in 1086. Barcombe is listed with 3.5 mills, yielding 20 shillings and held by William de Watteville from William de Warenne, the Earl of Surrey. Two watermills are recorded in 1572, and in the early 17th century there is a reference to 'the little mill of Barcombe alias Bardolfes Mill'. There were still three here in Victorian times. During the 19th century the mills produced flour and vegetable oil from locally grown crops. Another was a button mill, manufacturing buttons from what is known as vegetable ivory (no elephants or walruses involved). They utilised the nuts from the ivory-nut palm and similar species of palm imported from South America, in particular the Amazon basin, but also from trees growing along the banks of tropical rivers from Panama to Peru. The water-powered machinery was used to cut, shape and decorate this ivory-like nut, and what many people think are old ivory buttons are not.

At waypoint 3 are the surviving buildings of the station, built to serve the watermills and also anglers fishing for trout in the River Ouse. This was one of four stations on the Lewes and Uckfield Railway, which opened to traffic in 1858. Isfield is the next station north. The line closed in 1969, but little happened to the station buildings until the 1980s. Briefly a restaurant, the old station buildings are now homes.

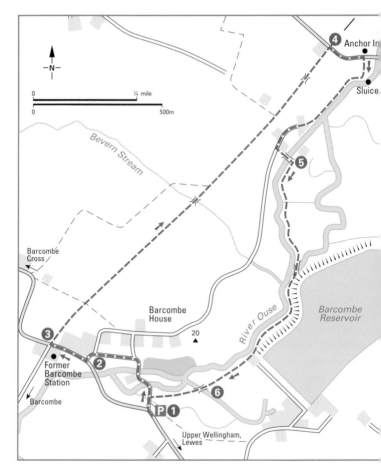

1. With the road on your left, find the path leaving the car park by an ancient oak to join a lane, where you turn right. Cross three bridges, the third across two sluices. Pass a list of tolls on what is reputed to be Sussex's first toll bridge, then turn left by houses on a metalled lane. For a few yards at the end this becomes a path.

2. Continue to the right on rejoining the through road to reach the former buildings of Barcombe railway station.

3. Here turn right onto a licensed bridleway, signed 'Anchor Lane', which heads towards the next station at Isfield. Follow the trackbed, cross a stream on a railway bridge and, where the main track bends left into a field, carry on forward past a modern house on a path through trees, soon ignoring a path to the right, still on the trackbed and over another old railway bridge.

4. Emerging at a lane, turn right. At the Anchor Inn, turn right into the car park. At the far end, go right through a kissing gate beside sluices and continue ahead along the river bank. Through a gate continue alongside a lesser branch of the river and pass a pill box. Emerge from trees by a pile of millstone fragments, and with the modern house passed earlier away to

your right. Go forward on a metalled track, past a barn, then immediately left over a bridge.

5. Turn right on the other side of the bridge, along the bank; the main river merges from the left at a kissing gate. Cross a footbridge, the path now along the opposite bank of the main river, the embankment of Barcombe Reservoir to your left.

6. Cross a footbridge. Carry on past a pill box and along the river, then go left along the lane back to the car park.

Where to eat and drink
The Anchor Inn is at the halfway point of the walk by the River Ouse. It serves food, and you can also hire rowing boats here. The Royal Oak at Barcombe Cross serves lunch and evening meals, and has a skittle alley.

What to see
Where you leave the trackbed of the Lewes to Uckfield Railway line at waypoint 4, look carefully at the road surface. Where the railway crossed the tarmac, the recessed U-section rails that kept the tracks flush with the road surface survive. It is ironic that the 'iron road' only survives where it crosses its great rival.

While you're there
A short drive east of Barcombe by the B2192 just beyond Ringmer, Raystede Centre for Animal Welfare doubles as an animal rescue centre and a free tourist attraction that is popular with families. It has wildfowl lakes, terrapins, aviaries, alpacas, an equine barn and even a zipwire. There's also a picnic area and a café.

ON THE SOUTH DOWNS WAY TO BLACKCAP

21

DISTANCE/TIME	8.5 miles (13.7km) / 4hrs
ASCENT/GRADIENT	902ft (275m) / ▲ ▲ ▲
PATHS	Footpaths and downland tracks
LANDSCAPE	River banks, woodland, downland
SUGGESTED MAP	AA Walker's Map 15 Brighton & The South Downs
START/FINISH	Grid reference: TQ417105
DOG FRIENDLINESS	Lead required where sheep are grazing and in town
PARKING	Brook Street Car Park, North Street, Lewes (pay-and-display)
PUBLIC TOILETS	Several in Lewes

The South Downs National Park encompasses Lewes, the largest town within a national park in England and Wales. The placid river scenery of the Ouse just north of the town and the Downs immediately outside create an abrupt transition into deep countryside.

From the river you look towards Hamsey's remote medieval church, on a tiny hillock. Later, from the Downs, you'll see Ashcombe Windmill, an exact replica of a six-sailed mill that blew down in 1916. You'll also pass close to the site of the 1264 Battle of Lewes, in which the rebellious Simon de Montfort defeated Henry III's men, leading to the beginnings of modern Parliament.

As you leave the river you'll see great chalk cliffs that are the result of quarrying activity for a chalkpit that was in operation from 1809 to 1880. Four lime kilns processed chalk into lime, which was used for a variety of purposes, including agricultural fertiliser. For the pit's first 62 years of operation, lime was transported by an ingenious method: a funicular railway operated by gravity. Trucks were loaded with chalk at the quarry, then let down a steeply inclined plane, with the weight of the laden carriages providing haulage for the empty ones that were on their way up to the top, where a large wheel at the top had a braking mechanism. At the foot of the slope, lime was unloaded at a canal (the watery ditch you follow from the river to the woodland), for shipping along the Ouse. The offices of the pit are now the Chalk Pit pub, and two kiln arches survive in the car park, together with the entrance to the railway tunnel beneath the A275.

The walk passes by what was one of the most scenic racecourses in the country, attracting crowds of up to 6,000 until its final demise in the 1960s. The Prince of Wales, the future George IV, is known to have attended races here, and the first such recorded event at Lewes was back in 1751, although a map of 1724 shows a 'horse course' on the site. Today the houses and buildings here incorporate the former grandstand, but racehorses are still trained on the Downs around here.

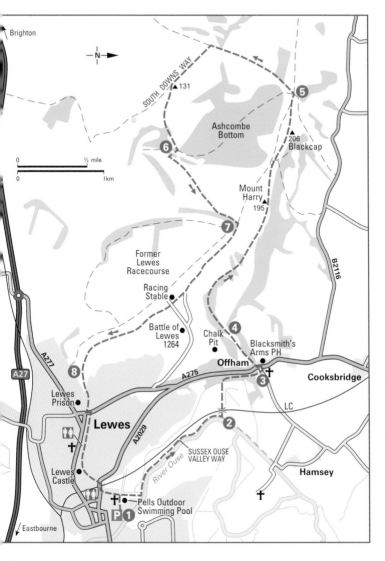

1. Leave the car park at the bottom corner, by the recycling bins, and follow Brook Street. At the junction with St John's Hill, turn right beside the L-shaped pond (a former millpond), passing the entrance to the Pells outdoor swimming pool. At the footbridge, do not cross but rather turn left on the Sussex Ouse Valley Way, along the river.

2. Just after a railway building marked 'Offham TP Hut', go through a gate and turn left under the railway bridge. Go along the field edge by a water channel, and through a gate into woods (the site of the foot of the inclined railway). Turn right on the woodland track. Eventually keep to the left of a pylon.

3. Emerge on the road opposite Offham Church, turn left and cross the A275 opposite the Blacksmith's Arms. Turn left along the pavement, then after

the last house (Toll Cottage) turn right into woodland, immediately forking right. The track rises steadily.

4. At the next waymarker go through the gate on the right (leaving the track) and follow blue arrow markers through the woodland, eventually rising to an open strip up on the left, along the edge of the woods. On emerging onto downland, go forward, keeping to the left of the nearest pylon, and pick up a path, through a gate and forking left up to the fire beacon on Mount Harry. Go along the top of the escarpment to the trig point on Blackcap, then carry on.

5. Just beyond a gate, turn left onto the South Downs Way. After a gate, fork left at a signpost. At the end of the field, between two gates, leave the South Downs Way by bearing half left along a fence on your right. At the fence corner carry on down, on a grassy path, to descend into Ashcombe Bottom.

6. Cross over the track and take the rising path half right opposite. Enter a field and turn left along the edge to a gateway, then half right to a gate on the skyline (to the right of the rightmost pylon). Carry on half right, eventually reaching a gate into woodland. Turn left.

7. Turn right at a T-junction with a chalky track. Descend past gallops and stables of the former Lewes racecourse. Keep ahead through a gate near the buildings, on a hard track which becomes a lane. Where this turns left, go ahead on the bridleway on the left side of a hedge. Ignore cross-tracks and follow this for 1 mile (1.6km).

8. At a T-junction near buildings, turn left, past the wall of Lewes Prison. Cross the A275, take De Montfort Road ahead, then walk down Paddock Lane. At the end cross by the Elephant and Castle pub, and go down St John's Terrace (which becomes St John's Hill), turning right at the bottom to reach the car park.

Where to eat and drink

The Blacksmith's Arms at Offham serves food and has a bar area as well as a secluded garden. Lewes has a full range of eateries.

What to see

Ashcombe Bottom is a wooded valley cut deep into the Downs, and its trees, scrub and glades shelter a variety of wildlife including white admiral butterflies, glow worms, badgers and dormice.

While you're there

On the other side of Lewes town centre, along the Ouse, is the Railway Land nature reserve (free access), reached from Railway Lane by Cliffe Bridge. An area of former railway sidings and water-meadows, it was rescued from a proposed supermarket development by a band of local nature enthusiasts and is now a prized nature habitat, with thriving populations of insects and amphibians as well as diverse plant life. Look out for the *Heart of Reeds* – a reed bed in the shape of a human heart, created by Chris Drury.

RODMELL AND VIRGINIA WOOLF

DISTANCE/TIME	3 miles (4.8km) / 1hr 30min
ASCENT/GRADIENT	75ft (23m) / ▲
PATHS	Tracks and riverbank path, village streets and some lanes
LANDSCAPE	Water-meadows of the River Ouse and villages on the foothills of the South Downs
SUGGESTED MAP	AA Walker's Map 15 Brighton & The South Downs
START/FINISH	Grid reference: TQ420062
DOG FRIENDLINESS	On lead along road between Southease and Rodmell and in Rodmell village
PARKING	In Rodmell's village street or at car park beyond Monk's House when the house is not open
PUBLIC TOILETS	None on route

In 1919 the novelist Virginia Woolf and her husband, Leonard, leading lights in the Bloomsbury Group, bought Monk's House in Rodmell as a country retreat. They were following her sister, Vanessa Bell, who had settled in 1916 at Charleston Farmhouse, near Eastbourne. Frequent visitors to Monk's House included poet T S Eliot and novelist E M Forster. A modest, weatherboarded cottage, it was extended by the Woolfs, and Virginia used a timber lodge at the bottom of the garden for her writing. Here she worked on her best-known novels, including *Mrs Dalloway*, *To the Lighthouse* and *Between the Acts*.

Besides the creativity of her writing and her life here with Leonard, Monk's House is inevitably associated with Virginia's suicide in 1941. Subject to depression and melancholia all her life, she drowned herself in the River Ouse. Leonard Woolf lived on here until his death in 1969, and Monk's House was given to the National Trust in 1980. Lived in by tenants, the house is open to visitors on afternoons from Wednesday to Sunday between April and October.

Southease's distinctive church has a round bell tower, one of only three in Sussex; most round towers are found in East Anglia, where there are about 170. Both areas are short of good building stone: round towers need no costly corners and edges in dressed stone, and they mostly date from about AD 1000 to 1200. At one time they were seen as defensive, a theory now displaced.

These marshes with occasional islands such as Lower Rise in the Brooks nearer Lewes were taken in hand in the 1530s by the local gentry, who channelled the river between dyke banks and cut drainage channels. The sea had invaded in the Great Storm of 1421 that caused enormous devastation and floods in Sussex and almost drowned Holland. Part of the drainage work included cutting a new channel to the sea, which emerged at a 'new haven' or harbour – now Newhaven, and not so new.

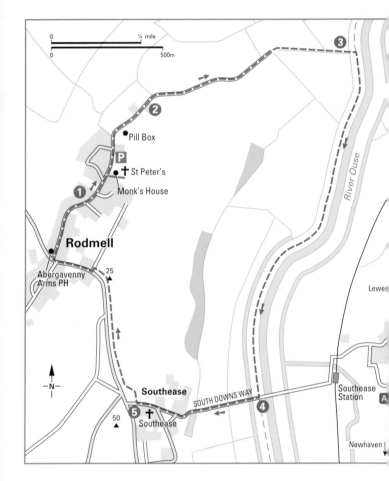

1. Walk along Rodmell's main village street, diverting to visit the church, and pass by Monk's House where Virginia and Leonard Woolf once lived. At the village/National Trust car park at the end of the village continue straight ahead (avoiding the road bending to the left) at the bridleway sign and onto a track.

2. Beyond a water treatment works you will find yourself in the flat water-meadows of the River Ouse, where it cuts through the chalk of the South Downs, with long views across to Lewes Castle and cattle and horses grazing. Continue straight ahead and through a bridle gate, most likely disturbing a heron or two as you go, then pass through another bridle gate to reach the riverbank.

3. Ascend the riverbank flood dyke and, through the kissing gate, go right to walk downstream, the tidal Ouse beside you. Continue alongside as it winds gently towards the sea.

4. After 1 mile (1.6km), emerge via a gate onto a lane by Southease Bridge and turn right. Follow the lane, and beyond a line of willows leave the water-meadows to climb to Southease, a small and pretty village with a green and a church with a Norman round tower and nave, and 13th-century wall paintings that were covered over for several centuries and restored in the 1930s. Continue on the lane uphill, keeping to the right of the church.

5. Halfway up the slope, and before this reaches the main road, take a gate on the right signposted 'Permissive path, Rodmell ½ mile'. Immediately go through another gate on the left and follow the path between fences, which runs closely parallel to the road and soon gains views across the valley. Beyond the next gate, this continues along the left field-edge. Join the road just after the 'Rodmell, please drive carefully' sign, on a stony path, then follow the road into Rodmell and the end of the walk.

Where to eat and drink
The Abergavenny Arms pub in Rodmell prides itself on home-cooked, locally produced food, and does Sunday roasts. By the church at Southease is a drinking water tap installed for South Downs Way users.

What to see
On the track out of Rodmell on the right is a brick-clad structure with a concrete flat roof amid willows. The slot openings for rifles and machine guns give the game away: this is a World War II pill box, one of over 28,000 mini-forts built in 1940 all across southern England to defend the country from a German invasion.

While you're there
Newhaven Fort, perched on the chalk bluffs above Newhaven, is open daily between mid February and early November. There is much to see, including guns, tunnels, ramparts and a recreated World War I trench. The current fort, built in the 1860s during yet another French invasion scare, is the last in a line of forts stretching back to Roman times.

THE VILLAGES AROUND ROTTINGDEAN

DISTANCE/TIME	5 miles (8km) / 2hrs
ASCENT/GRADIENT	305ft (93m) / ▲
PATHS	Busy village streets, downland paths and tracks, several stiles
LANDSCAPE	Rolling downland extending to the sea
SUGGESTED MAP	AA Walker's Map 15 Brighton & The South Downs
START/FINISH	Grid reference: TQ347032
DOG FRIENDLINESS	On lead in Rottingdean. Under careful control in places
PARKING	Free car park at Roedean Bottom, at junction of A259 and B2066
PUBLIC TOILETS	Rottingdean village and the Undercliff

Although just along the coast from Brighton, Rottingdean preserves its village character. It is one of seven Saxon settlements on this stretch of the Sussex coast, all ending in 'dean'. The word 'dean' or 'dene' means hollow or valley of the South Downs. 'The Deans' is the collective name for them and, apart from Roedean, the famous public school for girls, Rottingdean is probably the most well known. But there's a lot more to Rottingdean than historic buildings and landmarks, as a tour of the village will reveal.

Start the walk by following the scenic Undercliff, with its close-up view of the sea, then look for a comprehensive information board at the junction of the High Street and the A259, which helps you to identify what's what and who lived where as you explore the village streets. For example, the Black Horse was said to have been a meeting place for smugglers, while Whipping Post House was the home of Captain Dunk, the local butcher and a renowned bootlegger. Rudyard Kipling lived at The Elms in Rottingdean until driven away by inquisitive fans and autograph hunters. He wrote *Kim* and the *Just So Stories* here, among other works. Kipling loved the South Downs and he found these hills a great source of inspiration. Part of his garden is now Kipling Gardens, a beautiful park in the village centre, open to all. Some of Kipling's relatives had local associations, and it was here that his cousin Stanley Baldwin met and married Lucy Ridsdale, whose family lived at The Dene. Baldwin was a Conservative Prime Minister, who secured three terms in office during the 1920s and 1930s.

The flint church at Rottingdean is noted for its impressive stained-glass windows designed by the Pre-Raphaelite artist Sir Edward Burne-Jones, who lived at North End House. Enid Bagnold, who wrote the novel *National Velvet*, was also a local resident. From the green, the walk climbs up to Beacon Hill. The views are breathtaking as you make your way over this high ground, down to Ovingdean church, and back towards Roedean.

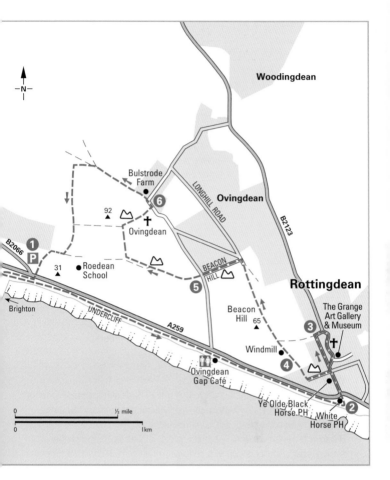

1. From the car park cross the A259 and turn right towards Brighton, following the path parallel to the road. At the metalled road on the left, go past the barrier and a sign warning pedestrians not to use the Undercliff in bad weather. Follow the road down to the Undercliff and head east towards Rottingdean for about 2 miles (3.2km), passing beside a toilet block. Continue on the path until you reach a group of buildings, including Highcliff Court.

2. Turn left into the village and pass the White Horse pub on the left. Cross the A259 into Rottingdean High Street. Pass Ye Olde Black Horse, Nevill Road and Steyning Road and continue along the street. As you approach The Green, look for The Dene and then Kipling Gardens on the right.

3. Follow the road round to the right and to a T-junction, then keep right and head back into Rottingdean village. Pass the war memorial and the village pond and look for the church on the left. Pass the Plough Inn and walk back down to the High Street. Turn left, then right into Nevill Road, climb quite steeply and bear right into Sheep Walk. Look to the right here for a good view of the village and its church.

4. Keep the windmill on your left and, forking left almost immediately, follow the bridleway along the downland ridge, carrying straight on at all subsequent path intersections. Woodingdean can be glimpsed in the distance, and the buildings of Ovingdean are seen in the foreground. The outline of Roedean School is visible against the horizon. Continue to a road named Beacon Hill, turn left and walk down to the junction.

5. Cross over to a gate, then go along the fence to a second gate. Follow the fence on the right which bends right. Soon after, cross to the other side at a gate and continue in the same direction uphill along the fence. Pass a private path to Roedean School and continue beside the wire fence to a stile in the field corner. Turn right and skirt the pasture to turn right over the next stile. Descend steeply towards Ovingdean church, cutting off the field corner to reach a stile. Cross into the field and keep the churchyard wall hard by you on the right.

6. Cross a stile to the lych gate and walk down to the junction. Turn left and, when the road bends right at Bulstrode Farm, go straight on along a wide concrete track, following the bridleway at a fork. Once well beyond the farm buildings, keep left at the fork, then immediately left again at the next fork a few paces beyond. Just after the track swings sharply to the left and is about to go up through a gate, keep forward alongside the fence on the left. The car park by the A259 looms into view now. When you reach the road, by the entrance to Roedean School, cross the grass to the car park.

Where to eat and drink

Along the Undercliff, you'll find the Ovingdean Gap café open at weekends throughout the year. In Rottingdean are several tea rooms, a fish and chip shop and a cluster of pubs, including the White Horse, ye Olde Black Horse and the Plough Inn. The last is nicely placed by the pond and serves locally sourced food and snacks.

What to see

As you descend to the Undercliff, look for the apartment buildings of Brighton Marina. Opened in 1978, this is one of Europe's largest purpose-built yacht harbours, with moorings for several thousand boats. Founded in 1855, Roedean School moved to its present site in the late 1890s from Sussex Square in Brighton. During World War II the school relocated to Keswick in the Lake District to avoid enemy attack. At various stages along the walk there are small stones to be seen beside the path, bearing the initials RS and the date 1938. There is no record of these stones in the school archives, though they might be some form of boundary marker.

While you're there

Visit The Grange Art Gallery & Museum at Rottingdean. Originally the vicarage, the Grange used to be the home of the artist Sir William Nicholson, who lived here prior to World War I. The building was enlarged by Sir Edwin Lutyens and now includes a gallery, museum and Tea Garden. Among the exhibits is a reconstruction of Rudyard Kipling's study.

ON DITCHLING'S DOWNS

DISTANCE/TIME	5 miles (8km) / 2hrs 30min
ASCENT/GRADIENT	600ft (183m) / ▲ ▲
PATHS	Field paths, bridleways and a stretch of road, several stiles
LANDSCAPE	Downland slopes and pasture
SUGGESTED MAP	AA Walker's Map 15 Brighton & The South Downs
START/FINISH	Grid reference: TQ326152
DOG FRIENDLINESS	Off lead on enclosed paths. On lead near Ditchling
PARKING	Free car park at rear of village hall in Ditchling
PUBLIC TOILETS	At car park

Ditchling is one of those picturesque villages that attracts generations of tourists, and it's a popular stopping-off point for walkers on the nearby South Downs Way. It shelters beneath the escarpment of the Downs, with rolling green hills and lush countryside enhancing its setting.

Over the years Ditchling's classic English village prettiness has attracted eminent figures from the world of theatre and entertainment. The 'Forces' Sweetheart', Dame Vera Lynn, settled in Ditchling; distinguished thespian Sir Donald Sinden spent his childhood here; and the actress Ellen Terry was a frequent visitor. *The Snowman* creator Raymond Briggs also lives locally. During the early years of the 20th century Ditchling became a fashionable haunt of celebrated artists and craftspeople, among them the cartoonist Rowland Emett and the sculptor and typographer Eric Gill, both of whom moved to the village. Another member of this illustrious coterie was the calligrapher Edward Johnston, who was widely admired for his revival of the craft of formal lettering. Johnston moved to Ditchling in 1913 and lived there until his death in 1944. His most famous work is instantly recognisable to just about everyone in the country – the lettering and logo for the London Underground, distinguished by a circle with a line running through it.

Ditchling's written records date back to AD 765. Sometime after that, the manor passed into the royal hands of Alfred the Great and Edward the Confessor. If time permits, take a leisurely stroll through Ditchling's streets and see the village at first hand. Its oldest building by far is the church, built mainly in the 13th century of local flint and imported Normandy stone. There are rare chalk carvings and a huge Norman treasure chest. During the Regency expansion of Brighton, the streets were busy with traffic en route to the resort. Horses were changed at the Bull Inn prior to the steep pull up on to the Downs. Make a similar journey on foot and you will enter a breezy world of wide skies and distant horizons.

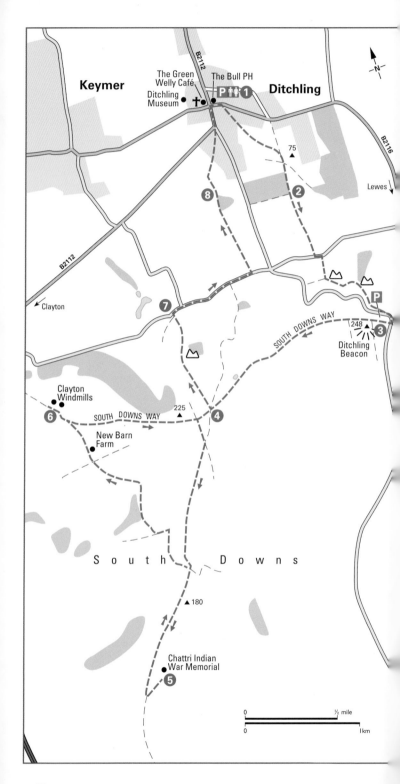

Keymer

The Green
Welly Café
Ditchling
Museum

The Bull PH

P 🚻 **1**

Ditchling

▲ 75

2

8

Lewes →

B2112

B2116

← Clayton

7

P

SOUTH DOWNS WAY

▲ 248 **3**
Ditchling
Beacon

Clayton
Windmills

6

SOUTH DOWNS WAY

▲ 225

4

New Barn
Farm

S o u t h   D o w n s

▲ 180

Chattri Indian
War Memorial

5

0   ½ mile
0   1 km

1. Turn right out of the car park and follow the B2116. Just after Charlton Gardens bear right, signposted to the Downs. The track divides by house No. 30: keep half left between hedges. Cross three pastures diagonally to the edge of woodland, walk along the wooden fence to a stile and join a broad path through the woodland. Keep right at the fork by a bridleway waymark post. Pass a house and go straight ahead alongside a beech hedge, where a concrete track runs off right.

2. Carry on along the track between trees, houses and gardens. On reaching the road, turn left and take the first track on the right. Ascend to a junction, fork left and climb the steep escarpment. Keep a breathtaking view of the Weald on your left. Further up, the path runs alongside the road. Look for the South Downs Way sign ahead and turn right across the road.

3. Skirt the right-hand side of the car park, through a gate and over Ditchling Beacon. Head west along the South Downs Way, avoiding side turns, pass two dew ponds and reach a major junction of paths. Hassocks is signposted to the right as a South Downs Way link route.

4. Keep ahead on the South Downs Way for a few paces and turn left at the sign 'Public Bridleway to Chattri Memorial'. Follow the path south, cross the downland to a gate and continue across the field to the next gate where there is a path junction. Keep ahead on the same path for some time, or until you spot the Chattri Indian War Memorial, unusually sited on the downland slopes. Turn left at a gate, and descend to this very atmospheric memorial, which was erected to commemorate Sikh and Hindu soldiers of the Indian Army who fought during World War I. For those who did not survive the conflict, Brighton Corporation acquired this remote downland so that proper cremation rights could be given in accordance with their faith.

5. Retrace your steps to the first path junction and turn left. Follow the field boundary to a gate in the corner and head north on an enclosed path. Turn left at the next gate and follow the bridleway down the field-edge. Make for a waymark and swing right, skirting the field. Climb quite steeply beside a golf course before joining the route of the South Downs Way on a track bend. Continue ahead and pass alongside the outbuildings of New Barn Farm. Follow the way until it turns sharp right and keep ahead towards the Clayton Windmills. Jack is a large brick-built tower mill which was worked until the early part of last century. Jill is a timber construction built at Brighton and conveyed to this site by teams of oxen in 1852. She has been carefully restored to working order.

6. Head back up the track, keep left at the fork and rejoin the South Downs Way. Pass the path taken earlier to the right and turn left just beyond it signed 'Hassocks'. Follow the path north, with a fence on your left, and soon it descends quite steeply through a hummocky area of old chalk pits.

7. Keep right at the signposted fork and make for a gate leading out to a lane. Bear left to the junction, then turn immediately right past a turning for Hassocks on the left. Walk along the lane, then take the waymarked footpath at the next stile on the left. Follow the path along the left-hand edge of the field, go through two gates by an eye-catching modern farmhouse. Continue ahead along the right-hand field-edge and go through a gap in the field corner.

8. Cross the centre of the next field to a further gap and a waymarker post. Follow the defined path diagonally right to cross a footbridge and then a stile and follow the path out to the road. Immediately bear left by a grassy roundabout and take the path to the right of the sign for Neville Bungalows. Cut between trees, hedges and fences, following the narrow path to the road. Bear right towards Ditchling and walk back to the centre of the village, turning right into Lewes Road for the car park.

Where to eat and drink

The Bull, in the centre of Ditchling, serves breakfast, lunch and dinner every day, using locally sourced and home-grown produce. The pub offers local beers as well as ales from its own micro-brewery. Directly opposite is The Green Welly, a café serving light lunches, pasties, cakes, tea and coffee.

What to see

Ditchling Beacon, although bleak and windswept in winter, is a delightful place. At 813ft (248m), it's the third highest point on the South Downs. The views are breathtaking and in good visibility you can see as far as the North Downs and Ashdown Forest. Now in the care of the National Trust, the Beacon represented one of a chain of fires lit to warn of the Spanish Armada in 1588.

While you're there

Visit the Ditchling Museum of Art+Craft, situated in the old school between the church and the pond. The history of Ditchling and its artists and craftsmen is illustrated in fascinating detail. Tools, country crafts and costumes are among the displays.

BY THE BLUEBELL RAILWAY AT HORSTED KEYNES

DISTANCE/TIME	5 miles (8km) / 2hrs
ASCENT/GRADIENT	230ft (70m) / ▲
PATHS	Field and woodland paths and tracks, stretches of quiet road, several stiles
LANDSCAPE	Peaceful woodland and farmland with views
SUGGESTED MAP	OS Explorer 135 Ashdown Forest
START/FINISH	Grid reference: TQ385282
DOG FRIENDLINESS	Off lead on parts of West Sussex Border Path (not allowed in ponds). Under control in vicinity of Horsted Keynes and railway station
PARKING	Horsted Keynes rural car park (free) by Horsted Club in village centre
PUBLIC TOILETS	Horsted Keynes station (seasonal) and village

There is something wonderfully evocative about the sound of an approaching steam train. Even standing on the platform of a restored station and gazing at the livery, the bookstalls and the adverts for seaside holidays can rekindle a host of cherished memories. Horsted Keynes station is just such a place, a railway enthusiast's dream come true. The station lies on the famous Bluebell Railway, a popular attraction since it came in to private ownership in 1960, with a section of line reopening within two years of its closure by British Rail.

Volunteers and dedicated members of its preservation society have played a crucial role in establishing, restoring and maintaining the railway. Being the first heritage railway to open in Britain, it managed to obtain an impressive number of railway-related items, including some wonderful period carriages that include a 1913 observation car, locomotives, old signs and station furnishings. The intention is to recreate a sleepy Sussex junction in the years before World War II. Although it's essentially just a museum recalling the heyday of steam travel, the station really does have the feel of that period.

Over the years the railway has featured in several television adverts, dramas and films. Its numerous appearances have included the films *Room with a View* and *Miss Potter*, as well as appearing as Downton station in the TV series *Downton Abbey*. The other stations on the line also have an enchanting period setting: Kingscote evokes the 1950s, while Sheffield Park, with its old station lamps and vintage enamel advertisements, recreates a country railway station of the 1880s.

For years the restorers' dream was to link the Bluebell Railway with the main network at East Grinstead once again. In the way, however was a mountain of household rubbish dumped by the council. After much money and volunteer effort that has now been removed and the line has been reopened. In 2013, the dream became a reality.

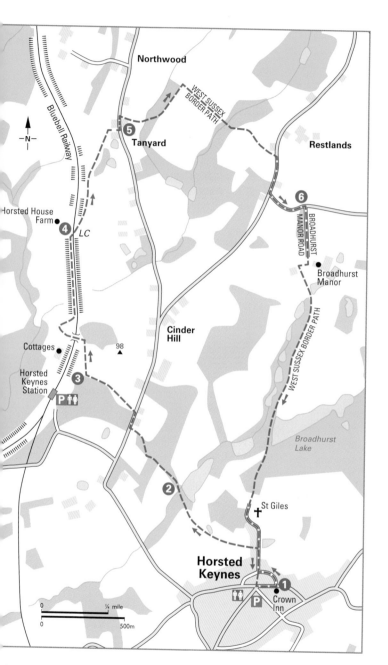

1. Opposite the village sign by the Crown Inn, go down Church Lane, bearing right downhill at the next junction and turning left immediately beyond a tile-hung cottage called Timbers, on a path between fences. Go through a gate and into the trees, past a pond. Beyond a kissing gate, reach a junction with a path

and continue ahead up a path that immediately drops to a junction by a signpost. Go straight over, past an angling club sign, and pass along the left side of a lake.

2. Just after a weir keep left at the fork, over plank footbridges. Carry on in this direction past a public footpath sign, emerge into a field and carry on to reach a road. Turn right on the road for 80yds (73m), then go left opposite a house on a signposted path between fences, skirting paddocks. Emerge on grass above Horsted Keynes station, and turn left to look at the station.

3. With the station on your left, walk up the track, keeping the railway line on your left. Just after the track veers left, cross the footbridge, turning right on the opposite side of the track. Follow the path as it heads away from the Bluebell Railway before quickly returning to the line. Turn left and walk alongside it.

4. At a footpath sign, cross the track to a stile, now keeping the railway on your left. Go over a minor lane (which goes over a bridge to your left), and keep alongside the right-hand edge of two fields to a gate. Follow the path across the pasture to the next stile and follow the path beyond.

5. Turn left on the road for about 60yds (54m) to a signposted gate on the right. Follow the path down the field and into some woodland, crossing a narrow walkway (care needed) along the rim of a pond. Turn left on the other side, up through the trees to a field, turn left and follow the path right, around the field-edge, and down to a gap in the vegetation and trees. Descend to a footbridge and go up to a kissing gate and field. Bear left and skirt the pasture to a stile and gate. Exit to the road, turn right along it, then left at the next junction into Broadhurst Manor Road.

6. Bear right at the West Sussex Border Path sign and walk along to the entrance to Broadhurst Manor. Veer right at the pond, still on the waymarked trail, which bends left, and follow the signposted track past a series of ponds to Broadhurst Lake on the left. Continue into Church Lane to reach the church of St Giles. When the lane veers right into Leighton Road, go straight on to return to Horsted Keynes village centre and the green.

Where to eat and drink
There is an excellent picnic area and the King George V buffet at Horsted Keynes station. In Horsted Keynes, the Crown Inn is a stone-built pub on the village green close to the Green Man; both serve food.

What to see
The Church of St Giles at Horsted Keynes is worth a look. In the churchyard is the grave of former prime minister Harold Macmillan.

While you're there
Take a trip on the Bluebell Railway before the walk or after it. One of the most popular destinations on the line is Sheffield Park.

CLASSIC CUCKFIELD

DISTANCE/TIME	5 miles (8km) / 2hrs 30min
ASCENT/GRADIENT	230ft (70m) / ▲ ▲
PATHS	Field, woodland and parkland paths, minor roads, several stiles
LANDSCAPE	Rolling farmland, attractive parkland and woodland
SUGGESTED MAP	OS Explorer 135 Ashdown Forest and OL10 Arundel & Pulborough
START/FINISH	Grid reference: TQ304246
DOG FRIENDLINESS	Enclosed paths and tracks suitable for dogs off lead. On lead on farmland and busy roads
PARKING	Car park in Broad Street, Cuckfield (pick up a parking disc, available in various shops on the High Street)
PUBLIC TOILETS	At car park

Standing 400ft (122m) above sea level, in the shadow of Haywards Heath, Cuckfield is one of those fortunate places that has largely escaped the threat of urban development, retaining its charm and character. It is generally thought of as a village, and yet it has the feel of a classic country town that has stayed small and compact – something of a rarity in Sussex these days.

It was the determination of the Sergison family back in the 19th century not to allow a railway to run across their land that saved Cuckfield from becoming yet another commuter town. The line was diverted to the east and provided the impetus for Haywards Heath instead.

Following the Norman Conquest, Cuckfield was held by the Earls Warenne, and was granted a charter in 1254. The pronunciation, 'Cookfield', unusual in southern England, stems from its meaning, the delightful 'cuckoo-field'. *The Clearing where the Cuckoo Came* is the title of a book of poetry about the village.

There are many notable buildings on the High Street and South Street, distinguished by a variety of architectural styles, but it is the famous tower and tall spire of the 15th-century Church of the Holy Trinity that stands above the rooftops of Cuckfield. From here you can look towards the Clayton Windmills, known as Jack and Jill, high up on the South Downs. The church, which has an unusually large churchyard, evolved from a chapel in the 13th and 14th centuries and was restored in the mid-1850s. There are various memorials and brasses inside; but the one feature which never fails to impress is the unique ceiling, which boasts a 15th-century framework with moulded bosses. It is thought to have been the gift of the grandson of John of Gaunt, who lived in Cuckfield in 1464. It was adorned with painted panels by a local artist in 1865.

Outside in the churchyard, by the Church Street lych gate, is a memorial 'in proud and grateful memory of those men of the 2nd Battalion Post Office Rifles who were billeted and trained in Cuckfield between November 1914 and May 1915 before joining the battalion in France and who never returned'. A stone's throw from the church lies Ockenden Manor, now a hotel. The name is Old English, meaning 'Occa's woodland pasture', and for several centuries it was owned by the Burrell family who improved and extended the building.

The walk begins right in the centre of Cuckfield, and after passing through the churchyard, with its views of the South Downs, heads southeast, then west across country to the little village of Ansty. A narrow lane leads north to Cuckfield Park, its open parkland enhancing this particularly attractive walk.

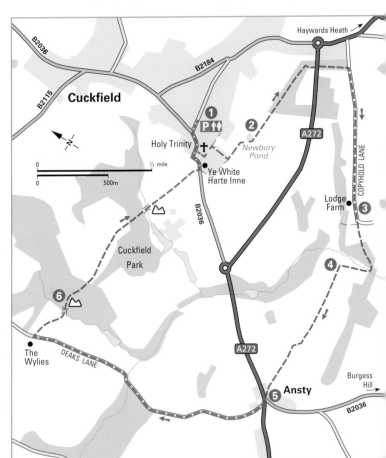

1. First leave the car park by turning left into Broad Street. Bear left again at the mini-roundabout and walk down to turn left into Church Street. Make for the lych gate by the parish church and enter the churchyard. Head for a kissing gate on the far side of the church, turn left and follow the track.

2. Pass Newbury Pond and keep ahead along the field boundary on the left before entering woodland. Carry on ahead to reach a signposted junction in front of some houses, and turn right. Follow the path on down to the busy A272, cross over to a stile and then follow the path through the trees. Turn right on reaching Copyhold Lane, later ignoring a left fork going to Copyhold House.

3. Pass Lodge Farm and, when the lane swings round to the left, carry straight on at the public bridleway sign, ignoring the path on the right by Copyhold Cottage. Follow the woodland path down to a lane. Continue straight on, cross over a stream and then immediately turn right to join a footpath, soon after crossing a footbridge. Once in the field, keep to the right field-edge.

4. At the field corner turn left by a signpost following the field boundary, and enter the next field via a gap in the hedge. At the end of this large field reach a footpath sign on the bend of a track. Keep ahead, passing a house on the right, and soon reach the A272 at Ansty.

5. Cross over and follow Bolney Road, turning right into Deaks Lane. Pass Ansty Farm and head out of the village. Keep to the lane for over a mile (1.6km) and, just after Cuckfield Cattery and a pond on the right, turn right opposite a house called The Wylies. Pass through a gap in the hedge and follow the High Weald Landscape Trail down the field.

6. Cross a stile and footbridge and climb steeply through the woodland, soon proceeding between fences. Leave the woodland by a kissing gate: this is the edge of Cuckfield Park. Cross a stile and follow the fenced path as it leads between trees and carpets of bracken, dropping down to a footbridge. Ascend a steep bank to reach a stile and keep the fence on your right. Continue to a kissing gate and then head towards Cuckfield's prominent church spire. On reaching South Street, turn left and return to the village centre.

Where to eat and drink

Cuckfield has Ye White Harte Inne on South Street, serving hot and cold meals and bar snacks, as well as the Cuckfield Corner House Café for light refreshments.

What to see

Cuckfield Park, established by an ironmaster in Elizabeth I's reign, was the home of the Sergison family. Later, it became a school and was open to the public. Now it is in private ownership. Keep an eye out for the striking gatehouse.

While you're there

You will identify several unexpected features in the centre of the village of Ansty. One is the Cuckfield Rural Parish Council map of rights of way in the area, which shows the full route of the walk, and the village sign shows a stag watching a horse and its rider trying to climb a hilly path. Not surprisingly, the name Ansty means 'steep path to hilltop'.

A BRIGHTON STROLL

DISTANCE/TIME	3 miles (4.8km) / 2hrs 30min
ASCENT/GRADIENT	164ft (50m) / ▲
PATHS	Pavements, streets, squares and promenade
LANDSCAPE	The heart of Brighton and its famous seafront
SUGGESTED MAP	AA Walker's Map 15 Brighton & The South Downs
START/FINISH	Grid reference: TQ311049
DOG FRIENDLINESS	On lead at all times
PARKING	Various pay car parks close to station
PUBLIC TOILETS	Several on seafront; Royal Pavilion Gardens

Brighton began life as a small fishing town, labouring under the name of 'Brighthelmstone', but it was Dr Richard Russell who really put it on the map in 1754 when he transformed the modest settlement into one of Britain's most famous resorts. Dr Russell believed fervently in the curative properties of sea water, and he began to promote Brighton as somewhere where the ailing could regain their health. Part of the cure included being towed out to the sea in horse-drawn bathing machines and plunged underwater by people employed as 'dippers'. It certainly caused a boom in the little fishing settlement, which became dubbed 'Doctor Brighton'.

The Prince Regent, who later became George IV, helped to strengthen Brighton's new-found status by moving to a house which he then transformed into the Royal Pavilion. The town's genteel Regency terraces and graceful crescents reflect his influence on Brighton. The Old Steine, an area of grass now dominated by busy traffic, became a fashionable strolling ground.

Later still, the railway era attracted visitors and holidaymakers in their thousands, boosting the town's economy to unprecedented new heights. As a seaside town Brighton has always been a mix of 'the raucous and the refined' as one writer described it. In 2000 the united boroughs of Brighton and Hove were awarded city status by the Queen, one of three 'millennium cities' to be favoured in this way.

Brighton changes in mood from one quarter to the next. The main reminder of Brighton's fishing-town origins as 16th-century Brighthelmstone is in a knot of picturesque tiny streets and alleys known as The Lanes, just in from the seafront. Further north is the area known as the North Laine, with its strikingly individual shops and funky cafés. West of the Palace Pier are Brunswick Square and Hove. To the east lies Kemptown, with its grandiose seaside architecture reaching a climax at the elegant curves of Lewes Crescent.

For sheer eccentricity, few buildings in Europe can rival the 18th-century Royal Pavilion, which looks stunning at night when floodlit. Even in the daytime, this Oriental fantasy, characterised by exuberant spires, minarets and onion domes, cannot escape your notice. Designed by the architect John Nash, it is Indian style outside, but inside the mood is of festive chinoiserie. Next door to it is the Dome, built in 1806, originally used as stables and a riding school for the Prince Regent. Across Pavilion Gardens, the Brighton Art Museum and Gallery is free to enter, and has an excellent section on the development of the town.

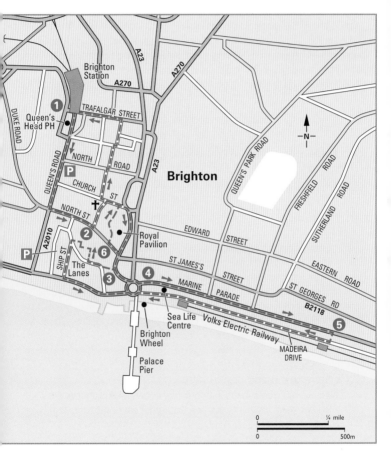

1. From the front of Brighton Railway Station, keep the Queen's Head on your right and walk down Queen's Road, heading for the sea. Cross over North Road and continue down to the junction with North Street. Turn left here at the clock tower.

2. Turn left into the broad, largely pedestrianised New Road. Pass the Theatre Royal on the left and on the right is the Brighton Dome Pavilion Theatre. Note the striking façade of the Unitarian church. Bear right into Church Street and pass alongside the Corn Exchange, part of the Brighton Dome. Keep the Pavilion on your right, pass the George IV monument and veer right. Just after three Art Deco bus shelters cross Castle Square into Old Steine and look for the YMCA and adjacent Marlborough House on the right. Originally built for the

4th Duke of Marlborough, the latter was sold in 1786 and later transformed by Robert Adam.

3. Turn right at some iron bollards and go along a pedestrianised walk simply called 'Avenue'. Cross over East Street and, just after the handsome town hall on the left (located in Bartholomews), bear right into Market Street, passing Nile Street. Continue into Brighton Place. You are now in the district known as The Lanes. Veer left opposite the red-brick former 1835 House of Correction into Meeting House Lane, turning right at the junction in front of the Friends Meeting House entrance and keeping left at the next junction. Just after the Bath Arms, turn left into Union Street, then left again into Ship Street towards the seafront where, after dark, you can see the flashing lights of a huge array of off-shore wind turbines. Veer left here and then continue to the Palace Pier.

4. Fork left by the Sea Life Centre and then follow Marine Parade. Pass Royal Crescent on the left, and the Madeira Lift on the right.

5. Opposite Bristol Court and Paston Place at a signpost to Kemptown, take the steps on the right, descending to the Volks Railway. Travel back to the terminus or return along the pavement to the Sea Life Centre, passing the statue of a local athlete, the Olympic gold medallist Steve Ovett. Cross into Old Steine, pass the YHA on your left and bear round with the road to the right, past Avenue, before turning left into Castle Square.

6. Take the second right through the India Gateway and the Pavilion Gardens and past the Royal Pavilion and Museum and Art Gallery to another ornamental gateway. Turn left. Pass the Royal Pavilion and turn left into Church Street. Turn right into Gardner Street, through the funky North Laine area, and follow signs to the station, turning right and immediately left at the end into Kensington Gardens. Turn right and then left into Sydney Street, and left up Trafalgar Street to return to the station.

Where to eat and drink

With over 400 restaurants in Brighton and Hove, and countless pubs and bars, there are numerous possibilities for eating and drinking along this walk.

What to see

The clock tower, at the junction of Queen's Road and North Street, was erected in 1888 to commemorate Queen Victoria's Jubilee the year before. The clock face has gilt Roman numerals and a gilt time-ball designed to rise and fall precisely on the hour. The Palace Pier is one of Brighton's most famous landmarks.

While you're there

Dating back to 1869, the Sea Life Centre is the largest in Britain, with many displays of live creatures. Alternatively, you can take a ride on the Volks Electric Railway. Built by electrical pioneer Marcus Volk and opened in 1883, it was the first public electric railway in Britain.

GRAND VIEWS FROM DEVIL'S DYKE

28

DISTANCE/TIME	2.75 miles (4.4km) / 1hr 30min
ASCENT/GRADIENT	656ft (200m) / ▲ ▲ ▲
PATHS	Field and woodland paths, several stiles
LANDSCAPE	Chalk grassland, steep escarpment and woodland
SUGGESTED MAP	AA Walker's Map 15 Brighton & The South Downs
START/FINISH	Grid reference: TQ269111
DOG FRIENDLINESS	Mostly off lead. On lead on approach to Poynings
PARKING	Devil's Dyke Summer Down free car park
PUBLIC TOILETS	By Devil's Dyke pub

Sussex is rich in legend and folklore, and the Devil and his fiendish works crop up all over the county. The local landmark of Devil's Dyke is a prime example, perfectly blending the natural beauty of the South Downs with the mystery and originality of ancient mythology. Few other fables in this part of the country seem to have caught the public imagination in quite the same way.

Devil's Dyke is a geological quirk, a spectacular, steep-sided downland combe or cleft 300ft (91m) deep and half a mile (800m) long. According to legend, it was dug by the Devil as part of a trench extending to the sea. The idea was to try to flood the area with sea water and, in so doing, destroy the churches of the Weald. However, it seems that the Devil might have been disturbed by a woman carrying a candle. Mistaking this for the dawn, he quickly disappeared, leaving his work unfinished. It's a charming tale, but the reality of how Devil's Dyke came to be is probably a good deal less interesting. No one knows for sure how it originated, but it is most likely to have been cut by glacial meltwaters when the ground was permanently frozen in the Ice Age.

Rising to over 600ft (180m), this most famous of beauty spots is also a magnificent viewpoint where the views stretch for miles in all directions. The Clayton Windmills are visible on a clear day, as are Chanctonbury Ring, Haywards Heath and parts of Ashdown Forest. The artist Constable described this view as the grandest in the world.

Devil's Dyke has long been a tourist honeypot. During the Victorian era and in the early part of the 20th century, the place was akin to a bustling theme park with a cable car crossing the valley and a steam railway coming up from Brighton. On Whit Monday 1893 a staggering 30,000 people visited Devil's Dyke. In 1928 HRH the Duke of York dedicated the Dyke Estate for the use of the public forever, and in fine weather it can seem just as crowded as it was in Queen Victoria's day. With the car park full and the surrounding downland slopes busy with people simply taking a relaxing stroll in the sunshine, Devil's Dyke assumes the feel of a seaside resort at the height of the season. Hang-gliders swoop silently over the grassy downland like pterodactyls and kite flyers spill from their cars in search of fun and excitement. But don't let the crowds put you off. The views more than make up for the invasion of visitors, and away from the chalk slopes and the car park the walk soon heads for more peaceful surroundings. Beginning on Summer Down, on the route of the South Downs Way, you drop down gradually to the village of Poynings, where there may be time for a welcome pint at the Royal Oak. Rest and relax for as long as you can here because it's a long, steep climb to the Devil's Dyke pub. The last leg of the walk is gentle and relaxing by comparison.

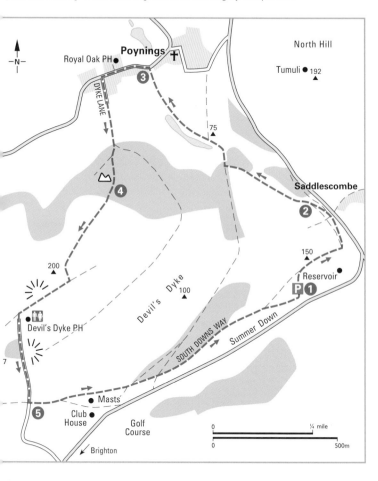

1. With the road behind you, take the kissing gate on the right side of the car park, go down across the grass for a few paces, then turn right on a path which you follow, soon passing a railing round a covered grass-topped reservoir. Soon the path curves left and drops down to the South Downs Way, which leads to a road. Part company with the South Downs Way at this point, as it crosses over to join the private road to Saddlescombe Farm, and follow the verge for about 75yds (68m). Bear left at the footpath sign and drop down the bank to a stile.

2. Follow the line of the tarmac lane as it curves right to reach a waymark. Leave the lane and walk ahead alongside power lines, keeping the line of trees and bushes on your right. Eventually veer right into the vegetation and cross a stile. Drop down into the woods and turn right at a junction with a bridleway. Past a pond, reach a path junction at the edge of the wood and fork left between fields and a wooded dell; go around a lake to a signposted stile. Turn right towards Poynings.

3. Head for a gate and footpath sign and cross the road, turning left along the parallel path along to the Royal Oak and then in to Dyke Lane on the left. There is a memorial stone here, dedicated to the memory of George Stephen Cave Cuttress, a resident of the parish for over 50 years, and erected by his widow. Follow the tarmac bridleway, and soon it narrows to a path. On reaching the fork, by a National Trust sign for Devil's Dyke, veer right and then fork left to begin climbing the steps.

4. Follow the steps up to a kissing gate and continue up the stairs. From the higher ground there are breathtaking views to the north and west. Fork right to a guidepost bearing purple and orange arrows, ignoring a left turn that rises steeply to a stile. Carry on to a kissing gate and head up the slope towards the Devil's Dyke pub, keeping it to your left. Take the road round to the left past the pub car park, walking along the footway beside the left side of the road past a bridleway sign, and look to the left for a definitive view of Devil's Dyke.

5. At a National Trust sign for Summer Down turn left on the South Downs Way. Follow the trail, keeping Devil's Dyke down to your left, and eventually reach Summer Down car park.

Where to eat and drink

The Royal Oak, located in the centre of Poynings, includes a patio and gardens for warm days and offers home-cooked specialities, local seafood, cask ales and summer barbecues. The Devil's Dyke pub, three-quarters of the way round the walk, has a family dining area and garden patio. Traditional British dishes, including Sunday lunch, are served and there's also a separate vegan menu.

What to see

Devil's Dyke consists of 183 acres (74ha) of open downland, which is home to all manner of flora and fauna, including horseshoe vetch, the Pride of Sussex flower and the common spotted orchid. The Adonis blue butterfly also inhabits the area. The Dyke lies within the South Downs Area of Outstanding Natural Beauty and is a designated Site of Special Scientific Interest (SSSI).

While you're there

Take a stroll through the village of Poynings, pronounced 'Punnings' locally. The village takes its name from the Poynages family, who held the manor here during the Middle Ages. Michael de Poynages, a one-time lord of the manor, left 200 marcs (£2,400) in his will towards the building of the 14th-century Church of the Holy Trinity.

BRAMBER AND BEEDING BRIDGE

DISTANCE/TIME	2.5 miles (4km) / 1hr 15min
ASCENT/GRADIENT	Negligible
PATHS	Riverside, field and village paths, some road walking
LANDSCAPE	Adur Valley flood plain
SUGGESTED MAP	OS Explorer OL11 Brighton & Hove
START/FINISH	Grid reference: TQ185105
DOG FRIENDLINESS	Take care on approach to Beeding Bridge and in Bramber
PARKING	Free car park at Bramber Castle
PUBLIC TOILETS	At car park in The Street, Bramber

Crossing Beeding Bridge, which is recorded in documents as dating back to the reign of Henry III, it is worth stopping for a few moments to consider its importance as a river crossing. Not only does the bridge play a vital part in this walk, allowing you to cross the River Adur easily from one bank to the other, but more than 350 years ago, in October 1651, it enabled Charles II, defeated and on the run, to escape his enemies and eventually flee to safety in France.

His route through the Adur Valley was one step on a long and eventful journey that has became an integral part of British history. Following the Battle of Worcester, where his army was soundly beaten, the young Charles fled across England, hotly pursued by Parliamentary forces under the leadership of Oliver Cromwell. Though documented fact, it has all the hallmarks of a classic adventure story – a colourful, rip-roaring tale of intrigue and suspense. First, he made his way north, intending to cross the River Severn into Wales where he could find a ship and sail to the Continent. But the river was heavily guarded, and Charles was forced to change his plans.

Instead he travelled south through the Cotswolds and the Mendips, eventually reaching Charmouth on the Dorset coast. Once again, his plans to escape by boat fell through and, in a desperate attempt to avoid capture, he made his way along the South Coast to Shoreham near Brighton, where at last he found a ship that could take him to France. His journey through England lasted six weeks, and during that crucial period he was loyally supported by his followers, many at great risk to their own lives.

The King's arrival in Bramber was one heart-stopping moment among many during his time on the run. As he and his escort came into the village from the west, they were horrified to find many troopers in the vicinity of the riverbank. Charles realised they had been posted there to guard Beeding Bridge, which was his best means of reaching Shoreham. Cautiously, he crossed the bridge and continued on his way undetected. Moments later, the royal party looked round to see a group of cavalry hotly pursuing them across country. Charles feared the worst, but as they reached him, the soldiers suddenly overtook the King and rode off into the distance. Fortunately for Charles, they had been pursuing someone else on that occasion. After their narrow escape in the Adur Valley, the group decided it was safer to split up and make their own way to the coast.

The accent is firmly on history on this very pleasant valley walk. Making for the Adur, the route follows the river to the bridge which Charles II crossed in the middle of the 17th century. The walk continues south by the river before crossing farmland back to Bramber.

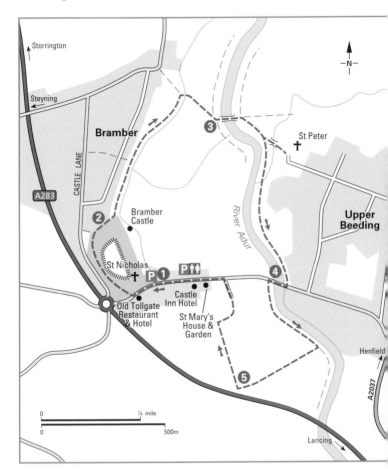

1. Facing the castle and the wooded ramparts, locate the narrow path in the left-hand corner of the parking area and follow it left as it meanders through the trees to the left of the castle ramparts. Keep right up the slope at a fork, then bear left sharply downhill to reach a track.

2. Turn right and head through the trees, passing galvanised gates on the left and right. The rooftops of houses and bungalows peep into view along here. Continue ahead at the next signpost and the River Adur can be glimpsed

between the trees on the right. Pass a footpath on the left and make for a galvanised kissing gate ahead. Follow the path on the right of the field to the next kissing gate and turn right towards the footbridge spanning the Adur.

3. Cross the bridge and bear right, following the riverbank towards Upper Beeding. Branch off left to a footbridge and steps leading up to the Priory Church of St Peter. Returning to the main walk, continue along the riverbank path towards Upper Beeding and Beeding Bridge.

4. Cross the road and turn right over the footbridge, then left along the right-hand bank, heading downstream. Continue to a waymarker and turn right down a slightly sunken path. Keep the fence on the right and, at the fence corner, go straight on out across the field.

5. As you approach the A283, turn right in front of the kissing gate and head towards the trees, with the ruins of Bramber Castle peeping through. Make for a kissing gate and bear right. Follow the track which bends left and, just before it bends right, turn left through a gate and right along a tarmac drive running through the trees to the road. Turn left, pass St Mary's House and walk along the High Street, passing the Castle Inn Hotel and village car park. On reaching the Old Tollgate Restaurant and Hotel, cross the road and follow the steps up to the church and car park.

Where to eat and drink

The Castle Inn Hotel in Bramber has a good menu with a choice of platters and mains, as well as pizzas, and serves breakfast, lunch and dinner. The Old Tollgate Hotel's award winning Carvery Restaurant serves a choice of locally sourced seasonal food.

What to see

Overlooking the Adur Valley and just off the walk is Sele Priory, established by William de Braose. Sele is another name for Beeding. The vicarage now occupies the site of the old priory, part of an ancient Benedictine foundation, and next to it is the Priory Church of St Peter.

While you're there

Before starting the walk, have a look at the ruins of Bramber Castle. Now in the care of English Heritage, it was built just after the Norman Conquest to defend the exposed and vulnerable Sussex coast. Nowadays, all that remains of it is the 70ft (21m) high gateway. Next to Bramber Castle is the Parish Church of St Nicholas, originally the castle chapel. Like the castle, this building also suffered in battle. Cromwell's men apparently used it as a gun emplacement, causing extensive damage to the nave and tower. Towards the end of the walk, you pass the entrance to St Mary's House & Gardens in Bramber. This splendid medieval building is one of the village's proudest features and the best example of late 15th-century timber framing in Sussex. One of the highlights of a tour of the house is seeing the unique trompe l'oeil Painted Room, decorated for the visit of Queen Elizabeth I.

CISSBURY RING TO CHANCTONBURY RING

DISTANCE/TIME	8.5 miles (13.7km) / 4hrs
ASCENT/GRADIENT	630ft (192m) / ▲ ▲
PATHS	Firm, grassy downland tracks
LANDSCAPE	Open downland, grassy ramparts of hill-fort
SUGGESTED MAP	OS Explorer OL10 Arundel & Pulborough
START/FINISH	Grid reference: TQ139085
DOG FRIENDLINESS	Lead required around grazing sheep
PARKING	Car park at Cissbury Ring (free), accessed from Findon village centre
PUBLIC TOILETS	None on route

High up on the downs north of Worthing, and connected by lonely, chalky tracks where you have little except sheep and skylarks for company, lie two very contrasting prehistoric sites. Both were supposedly created by the Devil when he dug up giant clods of earth in creating the Devil's Dyke near Brighton.

Cissbury Ring

Sussex claims 27 hill-forts, dating from around 100 BC to the Roman invasion in AD 43. Not all were definitely forts, although this huge one seems admirably suited to defence, surveying a view that stretches along the coast, across to the Isle of Wight and over the Downs. It would have housed a substantial Iron Age community, living in large thatched round houses, around which would have been pits and granaries for storing food. There would also have been places for ritual and religious activities, and animal enclosures as well as fields for growing crops.

Long before the fort appeared, this hill had been a major source of flint mining. This was in Neolithic times, over 5,000 years ago, when pits with complexes of radiating galleries were excavated by hand, using mainly red deer antler picks, and antler shoulder blades for shovels. The seams were about 40ft (12m) below the surface, and the filled-in shafts and waste tips from this industrial-scale mining can be seen all over the west part of the hill.

Chanctonbury Ring

Iron Age ramparts enclose the ring, with the site of a Romano-British temple inside. In your mind's eye you must add timber palisades along the top of the ramparts, to realise that the defences must have been even more impressive than they seem today.

Until 1987, Chanctonbury was one of the most prominent landscape features on the South Downs, topped by a huge clump of beech trees that could be seen for miles around. The great storm in that year blew most of it down, but it has since regenerated and one day it will be back to its former glory. Chanctonbury Ring has its own Morris dance team named after it, who dance on the site each May Day at 7am.

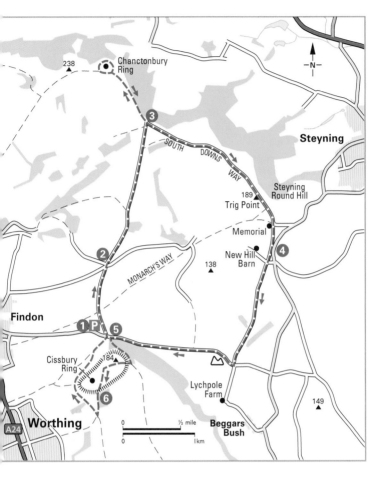

1. Turn left out of the car park, away from Cissbury Ring hill-fort. The track heads in a more or less straight line to the South Downs Way, periodically marked with dark red arrows. At the first junction, keep ahead.

2. At the next junction, generally keep ahead by avoiding a right fork, and keeping right at the next junction just after (avoiding a descending track to the left). Keep right at a fork where trees appear on the left. The track leads in a straight line, between fences. Later ignore a fork to the right, at a way-marker post.

3. At the junction with the South Downs Way, turn left along it to detour to Chanctonbury Ring, and walk round the ring itself to enjoy the huge views over the Weald and towards the Surrey hills. From there, return past waypoint 3 and continue on the South Downs Way for 1.2 miles (2km). Eventually pass a trig point in the field away to your right and the view opens up ahead, including Lancing College, the chimney of Shoreham power station and a huge abandoned cement works cut into the Downs. Keep ahead at a cross-junction by a memorial.

4. Where the South Downs Way goes onto the road, leave it and keep along the hard track, gradually descending. After 1 mile (1.6km) turn right at a complex of tracks, taking the second gate from the right, marked with a dark red arrow. This descends quite steeply. Ignore minor side turnings and carry on to the car park at Cissbury.

5. Turn left opposite the car park, taking the gate by the National Trust sign for Cissbury. Immediately fork left on the rising bridleway skirting to the left of Cissbury Ring. Near the top fork right and immediately right again, through a kissing gate and through the ramparts. From here there are huge views over Worthing, Littlehampton with its gas holder, and Shoreham with its power station chimney, and on a clear day you can see the cliffs on the east side of the Isle of Wight. At the trig point head towards a distant mast and follow the greensward.

6. Go through the south gap in the ramparts (with steps either side), and after a gate, go down, with woods on the left. At the corner of the woods turn right (signposted to Findon), generally keeping parallel to the ramparts. Near a National Trust sign take the left-hand of three gates and follow the path back to the car park.

Where to eat and drink

There is nothing on the walk itself, but Findon has two pubs – the Village House and the Gun Inn. Steyning, to the northeast of the walk, has a full range of eateries.

What to see

On this route you enter and leave Cissbury Ring via the two original entrances. The western half of the ramparts enclose most of the old flint mines, with a few mines and many spoil heaps outside. It is now owned by the National Trust.

While you're there

Free to enter, the Worthing Museum, in the centre of town, includes excellent displays of archaeological finds from Sussex, including a gold and silver Roman hoard unearthed nearby in Patching, as well as Saxon jewellery and a medieval logboat from the River Arun. It also has a notable collection of costume and textiles, from the 17th century to the present, and exhibits of local history.

HILAIRE BELLOC'S SHIPLEY

DISTANCE/TIME	7 miles (11.3km) / 3hrs
ASCENT/GRADIENT	98ft (30m) / ▲
PATHS	Field and woodland paths, country roads, several stiles
LANDSCAPE	Undulating farmland and parkland
SUGGESTED MAP	OS Explorer OL34 Crawley & Horsham
START/FINISH	Grid reference: TQ143219
DOG FRIENDLINESS	Off lead on drives and farm tracks. Under control through Knepp Estate Deer Park and near A24
PARKING	Small free car park at Shipley
PUBLIC TOILETS	None on route

It has been said that Hilaire Belloc is to Sussex what Wordsworth is to the Lake District. He was certainly passionate about the county, and this delightful walk suggests more than a hint of the great man's spirit. Belloc was a poet, writer, historian and politician – and exploring the picturesque countryside surrounding his Shipley home, savouring the beauty of the landscape, you really feel that you are following in his illustrious footsteps.

He was born in France in 1870, to an English mother and a French father. After spending much of his childhood at Slindon near Arundel, Belloc served in the French artillery. He then attended Oxford University, where he was an outstanding Union debater, much interested in history, politics and journalism. He forged friendships with some of the leading figures of the day, but also made enemies, including Herbert Asquith, Lloyd George and H G Wells.

Belloc is best remembered as a writer of more than a hundred works. Many were inspired by his extensive travels, with some of them describing extraordinary feats of endurance. He crossed the United States of America on foot to propose to a Californian girl he had fallen in love with when he was 19 years old. In later life he walked through France, over the Alps and down to Rome in an effort to meet the Pope. He failed due to an administrative mix-up, but recorded the journey in a book, *The Path to Rome*. In 1902 he made another marathon journey (albeit short by his standards) walking from Robertsbridge in the east of Sussex to Harting in the west – a distance of some 90 miles (145.8km), and wrote *The Four Men* – a reference to himself and three fictional characters who accompany him. It is written with the passion of a man who fears that what he most loves in the world is endangered.

Belloc bought King's Land in Shipley in 1906 and remained there until his death in 1953. The house was a shop when he bought it for the princely sum of £900. The walk crosses peaceful parkland to reach the village of West Grinstead (not to be confused with the much larger East Grinstead) and then crosses the River Adur to Dial Post. From here it's a pleasant country walk back to Shipley, passing Belloc's charming old windmill.

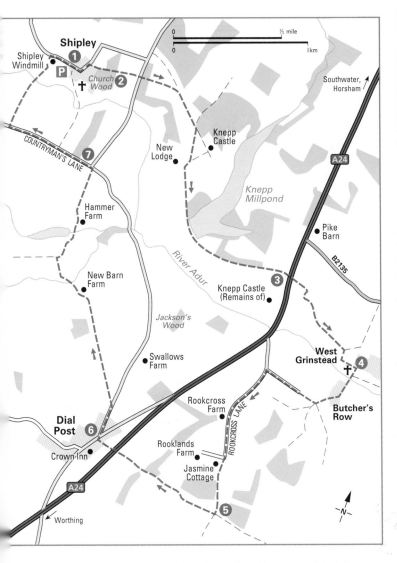

1. From the car park turn right and follow the road, Red Lane, round the left bend. After 100yds (91m) bear right through a defunct kissing gate and follow the right-hand boundary of the field. Look for a gate into Church Wood. Follow the path through the trees, ignoring the permissive footpath turns. Go through a gate and continue along the edge of the field to the road.

2. Cross over and follow a path through trees to a gate and enter parkland. Walk ahead across a field to reach a footpath fingerpost. Bear right and follow the drive towards Knepp Castle. On reaching a left turning, swing right and head across the pasture. On reaching a drive, turn right and pass New Lodge. Follow the drive as it runs alongside Knepp Millpond. The remains of the original Knepp Castle, designed by John Nash in 1809, can be seen across the fields.

113

3. Cross the A24 with extreme caution and locate a stile and gate just to the right of the bus stop. Walk ahead to a footbridge in the top right-hand corner of the field. The woodland path bears right and soon left by a stile and continues along the right-hand side of the field. At a hedge corner, with the roof of a house up ahead, go forward for about 75yds (68m) to a footpath sign and bear right. Follow the hedge to a gate leading into the churchyard, pass the church door and turn right at the footpath sign.

4. Make for a kissing gate situated in the corner of the churchyard and follow the paved path south. Cross the River Adur, bearing left to a gate and a concrete track which becomes a tarmac drive as it passes through the hamlet of Butcher's Row. Follow it in a southwesterly direction, keeping right when you reach a junction with two tracks and a footpath. Bear left at the next junction and follow Rookcross Lane. Pass Rookcross Farm on your right, go through a gate and keep to the metalled drive for 0.5 miles (800m), passing Jasmine Cottage, before veering right at a private drive sign to Hobshorts.

5. Follow the left-hand edge of the field to a fingerpost in the first corner. Enter the next field and turn right, keeping to the field-edge. Keep to the boundary, pass some oak trees, cross a makeshift stile, and drop down beside woodland to cross a plank bridge. Keep to the left boundary of the next field to a ruined stile in the corner and recross the busy A24. Cross a stile and an electrified fence and follow the footpath over pasture to a junction. Turn left, passing through the electrified fence and a gate into a field. Pass a bungalow and turn right to cross a rickety stile. The path leads to the Crown Inn garden and car park.

6. Turn right on leaving the pub, walk through Dial Post and veer left into Swallows Lane. Once clear of the village, branch off to the left and follow the straight farm road to New Barn Farm, where the track kinks left and right. Ignore a footpath turn to the left, and another further on, and continue along the track to the road.

7. Turn left into Countryman's Lane and pass a footpath that leads to the church. Continue to the next right-hand bridleway. Follow the path over two footbridges to Shipley Windmill, then continue to the main road and turn right for the car park.

Where to eat and drink
The Crown Inn at Dial Post serves good food made with local produce.

What to see
Although Shipley Windmill is no longer open to visitors, it may be viewed externally from the adjacent public bridleway. The largest windmill in Sussex, it was built in 1879 and acquired by Hilaire Belloc in 1906. He called the mill 'Mrs Shipley' and used to raise his hat to it. Following Belloc's death, an appeal was launched to restore it and by 1991 Shipley Mill was in full working order. The BBC filmed parts of the television series *Jonathan Creek*, starring Alan Davies, at the mill.

LOXWOOD'S FORGOTTEN CANAL

DISTANCE/TIME	4.5 miles (7.2km) / 2hrs
ASCENT/GRADIENT	82ft (25m) / ▲
PATHS	Field paths, tracks and tow path
LANDSCAPE	Gentle farmland bisected by Wey and Arun Canal
SUGGESTED MAP	AA Walker's Map 23 Guildford, Farnham & The Downs
START/FINISH	Grid reference: TQ042311
DOG FRIENDLINESS	On lead on road and stretches of farmland
PARKING	Free car park by Wey and Arun Canal, next to Onslow Arms, Loxwood, beyond pub car park and Canal Centre
PUBLIC TOILETS	Disabled toilet at Canal Centre

The Wey and Arun Junction Canal was completed in 1816 to connect the Wey and Arun rivers and form part of a continuous inland waterway route, linking London with the south coast. ('Junction' was later dropped from the name.) Glancing at derelict stretches of the 23-mile (37km) canal today, in places either completely dried up or engulfed by weeds and a sea of mud, you could be forgiven for thinking that 'derelict' is an understatement. But journey along the tow path a little further, and you'll see that a makeover is taking place.

After years of neglect, a great deal of restoration work has already been completed, and a stretch beyond the Onslow Arms has now been fully restored, with boat trips offered at weekends and occasional Wednesdays. To join together two sections either side of the B2133, it has been necessary to construct two new locks to take the canal underneath the modern road. But there is a great deal still to do if the Wey and Arun Canal Trust is to realise its dream of reopening this stretch of 'London's lost route to the sea'.

During the 19th century it was possible to travel by boat from London to Littlehampton on the Sussex coast via Weybridge, Guildford, Pulborough and Arundel. This route represented a tiny but important part of an extensive network of inland waterways covering England and Wales. To make that journey involved travelling along the rivers Wey and Arun, which were linked between Shalford in Surrey and Pallingham in Sussex by the Wey and Arun Junction Canal and the Arun Navigation. The canal was initially successful, until the arrival of the railway. It finally closed in 1871, and the waterway clogged up and was reduced to a stagnant depression in the ground, remaining in that state for the best part of a century. The lock by Devil's Hole, an abandoned oxbow of canal that was an earlier attempt to bypass a slope, was used by Canadians in World War II for target practice.

However, in the early 1970s a group of dedicated volunteers and canal enthusiasts formed the Wey and Arun Canal Trust, with the aim of restoring the canal as a public amenity, including its diverse range of wildlife habitats. Many of the original bridges and locks have been restored, but construction work of this kind is very expensive. The conservation project depends on fundraising and the goodwill of local councils, businesses and landowners.

This pretty walk begins in Loxwood, and gives an insight into the rebirth of the Wey and Arun Junction Canal, highlighting the various renovation works in progress. Heading north across lush farmland, the route eventually joins the tow path, and you'll see how the conservation programme is transforming the canal from an overgrown ditch into a vibrant waterway.

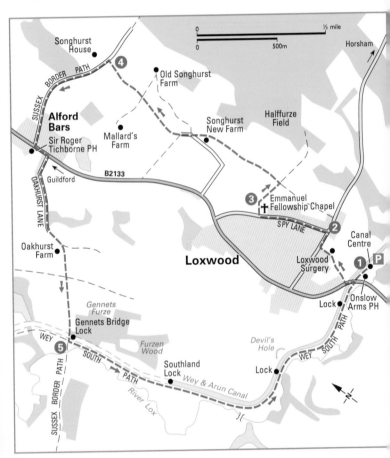

1. From the car park walk past the Canal Centre and the Onslow Arms to the B2133. Turn right and cross over the canal, continue along the road for 50 yards (41m) and then turn right along a signposted path which leads between hedges. Meet a road and keep ahead by Loxwood Surgery on the right. Turn right at the T-junction.

2. Pass Burley Close and turn left into Spy Lane. Follow the road as it leads between houses and bungalows and look for the Emmanuel Fellowship Chapel on the right. Bear right immediately beyond the chapel, through a gate, and skirt the Emmanuel Fellowship playing field.

3. Follow the path to a plank bridge and pass through a tongue of woodland. Make for the right-hand boundary of the field, then keep ahead to a gateway in the corner. Turn right and immediately left by a fingerpost. Follow the left-hand edge of three fields, passing Songhurst New Farm. Head for the field corner and look for a wide open gateway. Continue along a surfaced single-track lane, passing a brick-built house on the right. Continue for 0.5 miles (800m), passing a right turning to Old Songhurst Farm.

4. Turn left on reaching a T-junction with a lane, following the Sussex Border Path, and pass Songhurst House. After 0.5 miles (800m), turn left at a T-junction opposite the Sir Roger Tichborne pub along the right-hand verge of the B2133. Soon turn right along Oakhurst Lane, following the Sussex Border Path towards Oakhurst Farm. Approaching the farm, leave the lane on the left through a gate, as signed, and follow the track which bypasses the farm, ignoring a footpath turn on the left. Beyond the barns, the track heads on over a bridleway into an avenue of trees. Carry on to a new brick bridge over a canal at Gennets Bridge Lock.

5. Turn left here and follow the Wey South Path alongside the disused Wey and Arun Canal, which here appears as an overgrown ditch on the left. Continue on the old tow path, passing through several gates. Disregard any turnings and keep to the route of the canal. Pass the Southland Lock and then the Devil's Hole Lock and Bridge. Nearing the B2133, follow the path under the road bridge back to the car park.

Where to eat and drink
The Onslow Arms is characterised by its horseshoe-shaped bar. Food is served every day except Monday: pizza, ploughman's or sandwiches from the main menu, or cakes and cream teas. There are two beer gardens and a children's play area.

What to see
In Spy Lane is the former chapel of a religious sect formed in the 19th century. The adjoining burial ground is the final resting place of founder John Sirgood and 600 of his followers. Sirgood was a puritanical evangelist who came to Loxwood in 1850. He gathered around him the Society of Dependents, whose members became known as Cokelers, after a local field. The chapel is now home to the Emmanuel Fellowship, which has no connection with the Cokelers.

While you're there
Enjoy a summer afternoon cruise on the restored section of the Wey and Arun Canal. The weekend (and occasional Wednesday) trips begin by the Onslow Arms in Loxwood and last less than an hour.

PARHAM'S STATELY PARK

DISTANCE/TIME	5.5 miles (8.8km) / 2hrs 30min
ASCENT/GRADIENT	640ft (195m) / ▲ ▲
PATHS	Bridleways, parkland paths, and drives and stretches of road
LANDSCAPE	Elegant parkland and steep escarpment
SUGGESTED MAP	OS Explorer OL10 Arundel & Pulborough
START/FINISH	Grid reference: TQ069124
DOG FRIENDLINESS	On lead in Parham Park, in vicinity of B2139 and below Kithurst Hill car park
PARKING	Kithurst Hill free car park
PUBLIC TOILETS	Parham House (visitors to the house and gardens only)

The magnificent Elizabethan mansion of Parham House is one of the great treasures of Sussex, recalling the days of weekend house parties, servants below stairs and gracious living – a way of life that has all but disappeared. The wonderful setting, deer park and views of the South Downs enhance Parham's beauty, and little has changed here since Tudor times.

It was in 1540, at the Dissolution of the Abbey of Westminster, that Henry VIII granted the manor of Parham to Robert Palmer, a London mercer. Years later, in 1577, his great grandson, aged just two and a half, laid the foundation stone of the present larger house, which was built to incorporate the old one. The little boy's mother was a god-daughter of Elizabeth I, and it is believed the Queen dined here in 1593, on her way to Cowdray from Sutton Park in Surrey. The 875-acre (354ha) estate was sold in 1601 and then again in 1922, when it was purchased by the younger son of Viscount Cowdray. The new owners opened Parham to the public for the first time in 1948 – an unusual step in the lean, post-war years. The house has been open to the public ever since, and is now owned by a charitable trust.

Parham's gardens consist of 7 acres (3ha) of landscaped 'pleasure grounds' and a colourful 4-acre (1.6ha) walled garden. When the house is open, large quantities of flowers are cut from the garden each week for the arrangements which brighten the rooms. The herb garden grows medieval and Tudor medicinal and culinary herbs, while the orchard contains traditional varieties of apple and other fruit trees. Parham means 'pear tree settlement', but the fruit most associated with Parham is the Golden Pippin Apple, which is thought to have originated here in 1629. Of particular note in the Park are the many ancient, mature and veteran trees. A veteran tree contains significant quantities of dead wood or decaying limbs. Several oak trees are over 500 years old, and rare lichens flourish on the bark. A distinctive feature of the Park is the abundant mistletoe growing high up in the lime trees.

You'll see the house and Park from the top of the South Downs on this enjoyable circuit. Look out for the 18th-century dovecote when you walk through the Park. This has over 650 brick-built nesting boxes inside. Over the centuries, the pigeons would have provided the Parham household with a regular source of fresh meat, particularly during the winter months. Pigeon pie was a popular delicacy.

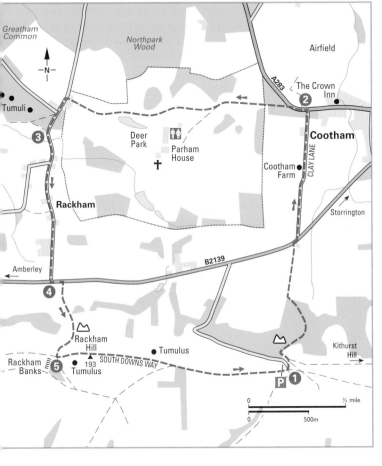

1. With the car park sign on the left, go forward to join a bridleway, which initially runs parallel to the road. Follow the path to a gate, cross a pasture to a second gate and follow the path as it descends quite steeply between trees and undergrowth. Ignoring a gated track on your right, keep ahead past rows of conifers. Join a track bearing left and soon turn right, passing alongside a line of trees, with a field on the right. Follow the track to reach a wooden gate leading out to the road by a house called Paygate. Turn right and then left along Clay Lane, passing Cootham Farm and Lower Barn to reach a junction with the A283. To visit Cootham and the Crown Inn, turn right.

2. Walk back along the main road past Clay Lane. Make for the entrance to Parham Park, pass a stone-built lodge and go through a gate leading into the deer park. Follow the drive and, when it curves gently to the left, join a way-marked parallel path on the right. Cross a pasture and look away to the south to take in a striking view of Parham House with the scarp of the Downs rising steeply behind it. On reaching a junction of drives head straight on, soon passing alongside a stone wall on your left with a lake beyond it. Continue through the gently undulating parkland and turn left when you get to the road by West Lodges. Pass a stone house and ignore a turning to Greatham and Coldwaltham on the right. Follow the lane down through the trees.

3. Pass a private car park on your right and head towards the dramatic scarp of the South Downs. Pass Rackham Road and follow the lane into the village of Rackham. Keep on the road as it cuts between fields to reach a junction.

4. Bear left here and, taking care, follow the busy and fast B2139 for about 75yds (68m). Turn right to join a bridleway and climb steeply, passing through a gate. Continue the steep ascent, crossing a farm track. Glancing back at intervals will reveal views of Parham Park in the distance and, away to the west, the meandering River Arun. The path curves to the right, and from this high ground much of the route of the walk can be seen. Amberley, with its imposing castle remains, is also visible from this lofty vantage point. Keep ahead to a bridle gate, ignoring a stile and gate over to your right, and join the South Downs Way.

5. Turn left along the South Downs Way ridge-top track and head east. Pass a trig point on the right and continue ahead across Rackham Hill. Parham House can be seen down to your left, while over to the right on a clear day you can spot the sea glinting in the sunshine. Pass through a belt of trees and continue to Kithurst Hill car park on the left.

Where to eat and drink

The Crown Inn at Cootham offers a good selection of snacks and main meals. Rack of lamb and game casserole feature on the menu, and there are cask ales and a beer garden. Parham Park includes refreshments such as light lunches and cream teas. There is also a picnic area.

What to see

The fallow deer here are descendants of the original herd first mentioned in 1628. The little church in the park, dedicated to St Peter, was built in 1545 and almost totally rebuilt between 1800 and 1820. The small village around the church virtually disappeared at the end of the 18th century.

While you're there

Tour the richly decorated Tudor Parham House, built during the reign of Henry VIII. The exhibition in the Ship Room shows the roles Parham played from 1922 onwards, and the restoration of the house: from fashionable country club to its role in World War II, and later as a home for 'mentally frail old ladies'.

ON HIGHDOWN HILL

DISTANCE/TIME	2.25 miles (3.6km) / 1hr
ASCENT/GRADIENT	82ft (77m) / ▲
PATHS	Grassy paths and well-defined bridleway
LANDSCAPE	Breezy hilltop with good views over downland and coast
SUGGESTED MAP	OS Explorer OL10 Arundel & Pulborough
START/FINISH	Grid reference: TQ098041
DOG FRIENDLINESS	Highdown Hill is good for dog walking
PARKING	Free car park and picnic area
PUBLIC TOILETS	Highdown Gardens

Rising 266ft (81m) above the Sussex coast, Highdown Hill is a popular recreational area and a superb playground for children, close to Worthing and Littlehampton. Here you can enjoy a leisurely stroll, enhanced by a wonderful sense of space and distance.

Highdown is a site of great archaeological importance. Evidence of Bronze Age, Iron Age and Roman occupation has been found here, as well as one of the earliest Anglo Saxon burial sites in England. The earliest permanent settlement was a late Bronze Age (c.1000 BC) enclosure. This was followed in the early Iron Age (c. 600 BC) by the construction of a hill-fort, composed of a single rampart and ditch. Subsequently the site was used as an Anglo Saxon burial ground, c. AD 450. It was discovered quite by accident in the late 19th century, when a local landowner was carrying out some tree planting inside the hill-fort. Excavations that followed between 1893 and 1894 uncovered 86 Anglo-Saxon graves. Most of the objects that were found, which include an unusual number of glass ones, are now on display in Worthing Museum.

In 1588 a beacon was lit here to warn of the approaching Spanish Armada, and during World War II a radar station was built on the hill, causing considerable damage to the site during its construction. The great storm of 1987 caused further damage, uprooting many trees, and a rescue dig took place the following year. Today Highdown is in the care of the National Trust.

Highdown Hill's grassland includes a number of important wildlife habitats. Plants most closely associated with the old chalk grazing land include cowslip, kidney vetch, chalk milkwort and common spotted orchid. The Carthusian snail, a rare mollusc, has been discovered here, and birds such as linnet, goldfinch and willow warbler are known to inhabit the area.

This short, airy walk – combined with a visit to nearby Highdown Gardens – provides a rewarding half-day out. You might also like to call in at Highdown Vineyard, situated on the southern slope of the hill, and accessed from the A259, not far from the turn-off to Highdown Hill. There's a shop and tea room there, and wine tastings and tours can also be arranged.

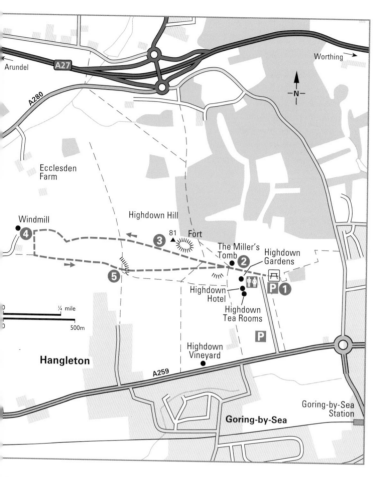

1. With your back to the coast, follow the path from the top left-hand corner of the car park, immediately curving left. Keep ahead on the main path, passing a clump of bushes on your right, then veer right to the Miller's Tomb. Pass the tomb and go through the gate to an interpretation board recording the fascinating history of Highdown Hill.

2. Stride out along the top of the ridge over the hill, keeping the trees on your right. The remains of the hill-fort and its grassy earthworks can be seen now. To the right, at the western end of the site, you'll see a trig point.

3. Descend gently to a gate and then go straight ahead in the next field. The stump of Ecclesden Windmill, minus its sails, can be seen in the distance. Soon the path curves to the right and hugs the field boundary, passing a track running off to the right. Maintain the same westerly direction and keep the field boundary on your right. Make for the field corner, turning left to follow the path between fences.

4. The old windmill lies to your right now. Continue ahead to reach a junction with a bridleway. Turn left here and follow the path which leads between

bushes and margins of vegetation. Eventually you reach steps on the left. Disregard them, and no more than 10 paces beyond the steps you arrive at a junction of bridleways.

5. Keep left here, by the National Trust 'Highdown Hill' sign, and follow the track up the slope between the bushes. Very quickly you will reach the exposed, lower slopes of Highdown Hill, following its contours in an easterly direction. Avoid the paths running up the hill and pass a fenced field on the right. Continue on the main path to reach a signpost. Fork right to keep ahead here towards the trees, rejoining the outward route at the interpretation board. Go through the gate, pass the Miller's Tomb and retrace your steps to the car park.

Where to eat and drink

Highdown Tea Rooms, open every day throughout the year, offers rolls, sandwiches, salads, cakes and cream teas. Next door is Highdown Hotel, which includes two bars, a family restaurant and a carvery restaurant. Light snacks, jacket potatoes and more substantial main courses are available, as is a children's menu.

What to see

The Miller's Tomb contains the remains of John Oliver, an eccentric 18th-century miller, who allegedly had the tomb constructed on Highdown Hill more than 20 years before his death. The reason? So that smuggler Oliver could store contraband safely and in the least likely place. He died in 1793.

While you're there

Visit Highdown's lovely chalk garden, which is open throughout the year and was established by Sir Frederick and Lady Stern, who worked for 50 years to prove that plants would grow on chalk. The garden was created out of a disused chalk pit at a time when horticulturalists were travelling to China and the Himalayan regions to collect rare and beautiful plants. Many of the original species from those early expeditions survive in the garden today. Following Sir Frederick's death in 1967, his widow left the garden to Worthing Borough Council.

CLIMPING – COUNTRYSIDE MEETS COAST

DISTANCE/TIME	4 miles (6.4km) / 2hrs
ASCENT/GRADIENT	Negligible
PATHS	Field paths, roads and stretches of beach
LANDSCAPE	Sandy beaches, open farmland and riverside development
SUGGESTED MAP	AA Walker's Map 20 Chichester & The South Downs
START/FINISH	Grid reference: TQ005007
DOG FRIENDLINESS	Off lead on enclosed paths and beach area. Under control near the Arun and on road at Climping
PARKING	Fee-paying car park at Climping Beach
PUBLIC TOILETS	Climping Beach

Much of the Sussex coast has grown and evolved since early pioneering photographers captured classic seaside scenes at Worthing, Hove and Littlehampton, and now a chain of urban development extends almost continuously from Bognor to Brighton. Here and there are still hints of the coastline as it used to be before the builders moved in, but Climping Beach, where this walk begins, is an altogether different place. There is a feeling of space and distance here, rarely experienced on the West Sussex coast.

One of Climping's main attractions is its remoteness. It is approached along a country lane which terminates at the beach car park. A glance at a map of this area might cause some confusion. The village of Climping, which has a 13th-century church, lies a mile (1.6km) or so inland, and the nearest settlement to Climping Beach is Atherington. The medieval church and various dwellings of this old parish now lie beneath the sea, which has steadily encroached upon the land, and all that is now left of low-lying Atherington are several houses and a hotel.

Climping Beach, together with neighbouring West Beach, is popular with holidaymakers as well as locals who want to enjoy the space. The National Trust protects more than 2 miles (3.2km) of coastline here. The low-water, sandy beach is backed by shingle banks which, in places, support vegetation, a rare habitat in Britain. In addition, there are active sand dunes, which are another rare and fragile feature of the coastline. Only six areas of active sand dunes survive on the south coast between Cornwall and Kent, and three of them are in Sussex. After crossing a broad expanse of flat farmland, the walk eventually reaches the River Arun, opposite Littlehampton. From here it's a pleasant amble to West Beach, finishing with a spectacular stroll by the sea, back to Climping Beach. There is much to divert the attention along the way, but it is this lonely stretch of coastline that makes the greatest impression – a vivid reminder of how the entire West Sussex coast once looked.

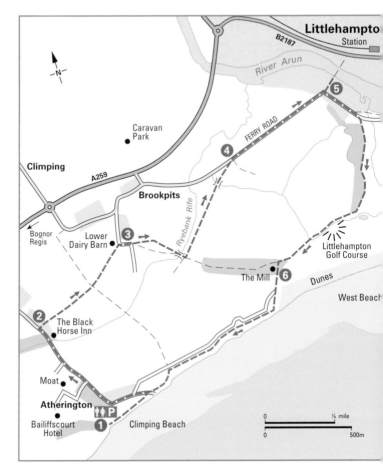

1. From the beach car park take the road leading away from the sea, passing the entrance to Bailiffscourt Hotel on the left-hand side. Continue walking along the road until you reach The Black Horse Inn, and take the next footpath on the right, by some thatched cottages.

2. When the track swings left, continue ahead across the field to a signpost at a junction with a byway. Go straight over and follow the path through the fields towards a tile-roofed barn.

3. At the building, Lower Dairy Barn, join a grassy track on a bend beside a traditional Sussex flint wall and gable, and turn right along it. As it swings right, take the signposted path and begin by following the boundary hedge. Stride out across the field, cross the concrete footbridge and bear left at the footpath sign to follow a deep ditch known as the Ryebank Rife. At a signpost, veer away from the ditch and cross the field to a line of trees, aiming towards a distant pale blue gasometer. Cross a footbridge to the road.

4. Turn right and walk along the pavement to a turning on the right for Littlehampton Golf Course. The walk follows this road, but first continue ahead

for a few steps to have a look at the footbridge crossing the Arun. The buildings of Littlehampton can be seen on the far side and, if time allows, you may like to extend the walk by visiting the town.

5. Continuing the main walk, follow the road towards West Beach and the golf course, veering right at a car park sign to follow an enclosed path to a kissing gate at the corner of the golf course. Continuing ahead, the path (which can be very muddy) runs along a raised bank through trees and later emerges into the open with good views over this unspoilt coastal plain. Keep to the path, and at the end of the golf course you reach a flint-built house. Avoid the path on the right here and keep left.

6. Continue walking along the footpath, which soon reaches West Beach. Look for the interpretation board, which explains how this open stretch of coastline has been shaped and influenced by climatic conditions and the sea over the centuries. Follow the footpath ahead along the edge of the shingle beach (be aware that the road that runs parallel to it below is private) back to the car park. When the tide is out you can walk along the sand instead.

Where to eat and drink

The Black Horse Inn near Climping Beach is located on the route of the walk and is an ideal stop if you're completing it on a summer's evening. Eat and drink outside or relax in the cosy bar. The inn offers a range of ales and a wide selection of hot and cold food. Littlehampton has a good choice of pubs, including several in the vicinity of the Arun.

What to see

As you begin the walk, look for the entrance to Bailiffscourt Hotel. Roger de Montgomery, William the Conqueror's cousin, permitted Benedictine monks from the Abbey of Seez to establish a chapel at Climping. Their bailiff occupied what is now the hotel. The building was later remodelled in the authentic medieval style.

While you're there

Read about the history of the bridge over the Arun. The river, which is fast-flowing and reaches up to 7 knots during the spring tides, effectively separates the town of Littlehampton from the adjoining countryside. The view downstream from the bridge is of various boatyards and Docklands-style warehouses which have been converted into apartments. Littlehampton was a thriving port during the Middle Ages, when stone from Normandy was landed here for the construction of many of the county's churches and castles. Later, it became a fashionable seaside resort with its seafront lined by striking Victorian and Edwardian villas.

AN ARUNDEL CASTLE LOOP

DISTANCE/TIME	3.25 miles (5.3km) / 3hrs
ASCENT/GRADIENT	305ft (93m) / ▲ ▲
PATHS	Riverside and parkland paths, some road walking, 1 stile
LANDSCAPE	Valley, rolling parkland and town
SUGGESTED MAP	AA Walker's Map 20 Chichester & The South Downs
START/FINISH	Grid reference: TQ020071
DOG FRIENDLINESS	Off lead on tow path. Not permitted in Arundel Park. Final stage of the walk is along busy roads in Arundel
PARKING	Mill Road fee-paying car park, Arundel
PUBLIC TOILETS	At car park in Mill Road; Swanbourne Lake
NOTES	Arundel Park is closed annually on 24 March

Arundel has rows of elegant Georgian and Victorian buildings, fine shops and a picturesque riverside setting, but topping the list of attractions is surely the town's magnificent castle. As you drive along the A27 to the south of Arundel, its great battlements, together with the grandiose French Gothic-style Roman Catholic cathedral, can be seen dwarfing the town's other buildings.

There has been a castle here since the 11th century, though most of the present fortification is Victorian. Arundel Castle is the principal ancestral home of the Dukes of Norfolk, formerly the Earls of Arundel. There are various family portraits inside the castle, some of them believed to date back to the Wars of the Roses. The Norfolks have lived at Arundel since the 16th century. According to the plaque at the bottom of the High Street: 'Since William Rose and Harold fell, There have been Earls at Arundel'.

The castle was attacked by Parliamentary forces during the Civil War. However, it was extensively rebuilt and restored in the 18th and 19th centuries. Within its great walls lies a treasure trove of sumptuous riches, including a fascinating collection of fine furniture dating from the 16th century, tapestries, clocks and portraits by Van Dyck, Gainsborough, Reynolds, Mytens and Lawrence, among others. Personal items belonging to Mary, Queen of Scots and an assortment of religious and heraldic items from the Duke of Norfolk's collection can also be viewed.

The walk starts down by the Arun, and from here there are teasing glimpses of the castle, but it is not until you have virtually finished the walk that you reach its main entrance, saving the best until last. Following the riverbank through the tranquil Arun Valley, renowned for its bird life, the walk eventually reaches Arundel Park, a delight in any season. Swanbourne Lake, a great attraction for young children, lies by the entrance to the park, making it easily accessible for everyone. However, once the bustling lake scene fades from view, the park assumes a totally different character. Rolling hills and tree-clad slopes crowd in from every direction and only occasional serious walkers are likely to be seen in these more remote surroundings. You may feel isolated, briefly cut off the from the rest of the world at this point, but the interlude is soon over when you find yourself back in Arundel. Pass the huge edifice of the cathedral, built in 1870, and make your way down to the castle entrance. Walk down the High Street, said to be the steepest in England, and by the bridge at the bottom you can see the remains of the Blackfriars monastery, dissolved in 1546 by Henry VIII.

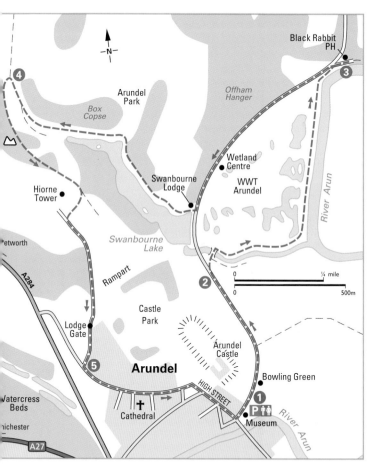

1. From the car park on Mill Road, turn right and walk along the tree-lined pavement. Pass the bowling green, and a glance to your left will reveal a dramatic view of historic Arundel Castle with its imposing battlements.

2. Follow the road to the elegant stone bridge, avoid the first path on the right and cross over via a footbridge, and turn right to join the riverside path, partly shaded by overhanging trees. Continue along this, emerging from the trees to reach the western bank of the Arun. Turn left here and walk beside the

reed-fringed Arun to the Black Rabbit pub, which can be seen standing out against a curtain of trees.

3. From the Black Rabbit, turn left on the minor road back towards Arundel, passing the entrance to the WWT Arundel Wetland Centre. About 300yds (274m) beyond the Centre pass through a gate on the right leading into Arundel Park past Swanbourne Lodge, and follow the path alongside Swanbourne Lake. Eventually the lake fades from view as the walk reaches deeper into the park. Ignore a turning branching off to the left, just before a kissing gate, and follow the path as it curves gently to the right.

4. Turn sharply to the left at the next waymarked junction and begin a fairly steep ascent, with the footpath through the park seen curving away down to the left, back towards the lake. This stretch of the walk offers glorious views over elegant Arundel Park. The path becomes faint as it passes the corner of the wood. Carry straight on, climbing all the time, then aim for a stile and gate when they come into view. After the stile, bear immediately right up some steps. Cross the grass, following the waymarks and keeping to the left of Hiorne Tower. On reaching a driveway, turn left and walk down to Park Lodge. Keep to the right by the private drive and make for the road.

5. Turn left, pass Arundel Cathedral and bear left at the road junction by the entrance to Arundel Castle. Go down the hill, back into the centre of Arundel. You'll find Mill Road at the bottom of the High Street.

Where to eat and drink

Arundel offers a good choice of places to eat and drink. The Black Rabbit at Offham, on the route of the walk, is delightfully situated on the Arun. Cheerful hanging baskets add plenty of colour in summer when you can sit outside and relax in these very attractive surroundings. The WWT Arundel Wetland Centre has a café by the water's edge, and there are tea rooms at Swanbourne Lodge serving cream teas and a variety of tempting cakes.

What to see

Climbing up from Arundel Park brings you to Hiorne Tower, a remote but beautifully situated folly. Triangular in plan and recently restored, the folly was built by Francis Hiorne in an effort to ingratiate himself with the then Duke of Norfolk so that he might work on the restoration of Arundel Castle. The duke agreed to engage him on the restoration, but Hiorne died before he could begin work.

While you're there

Visit the Wildfowl and Wetlands Trust's Arundel Wetland Centre, which is situated directly on the route of the walk. There are many attractions to divert your attention. Ducks, geese and swans from all over the world make their home here, and the popular boardwalk enables you to explore one of the largest reed beds in Sussex. Arundel's new, purpose-built museum, situated next door to the car park in Mill Road, features displays about the castle, town and river.

AN AMBERLEY DOWNLAND RAMBLE

DISTANCE/TIME	6.5 miles (10.5km) / 3hrs 20min
ASCENT/GRADIENT	800ft (244m) / ▲ ▲ ▲
PATHS	Riverside paths, downland tracks and some roads, several stiles
LANDSCAPE	Arun Valley and downland
SUGGESTED MAP	AA Walker's Map 20 Chichester & The South Downs
START/FINISH	Grid reference: TQ026118
DOG FRIENDLINESS	Keep on lead heading up Camp Hill to safeguard ground-nesting birds. Off lead on other stretches of downland and riverside
PARKING	Free parking for rail users at Amberley Station, or adjoining car park for visitors to the museum
PUBLIC TOILETS	Amberley Museum & Heritage Centre

This invigorating downland walk begins where reality meets nostalgia. Visiting an old chalk quarry at the start of the route, you have the chance to forget the modern world, step into the past and recall a way of life that has long vanished. Amberley is a charming, tranquil village with a history going back to medieval times, and was the summer residence of the Bishops of Chichester.

Amberley Museum & Heritage Centre is well worth a visit, entered via the Amberley railway station car park. The open-air museum, which covers 36 acres (15ha) of a long-disused chalk pit in the Arun Valley, was opened in 1979. Its objective is to illustrate how the traditional industries of southeast England evolved during the 19th and 20th centuries. Few museums thrill and excite adults and children alike as much as this one does. To prove it, there are almost 100,000 visitors a year.

Visit the bus garage and the signwriter's workshop, the locomotive shed, the village blacksmith's, stop at the telephone exchange or discover the wheelwright's shop. You may meet skilled craftspeople from the museum's resident team exercising ancient trades. Using traditional materials and tools, they produce a choice of fine wares, which enables them to earn a living and keep their trade thriving. Elsewhere, exhibits are demonstrated by volunteers, many of whom have acquired a lifetime of experience in their trade.

One of the highlights of a visit to the Amberley Museum & Heritage Centre is a trip around the site on board a vintage bus, or perhaps a tour on the narrow-gauge railway. The train ride takes visitors between Amberley and Brockham stations, and yet never leaves the museum site. When you finally leave the museum, follow the River Arun and begin the gradual climb into the hills. Up here, with its wide-open skies and far-ranging views, you can feel the bracing wind in your face as you explore some of the loneliest tracts of downland anywhere in Sussex.

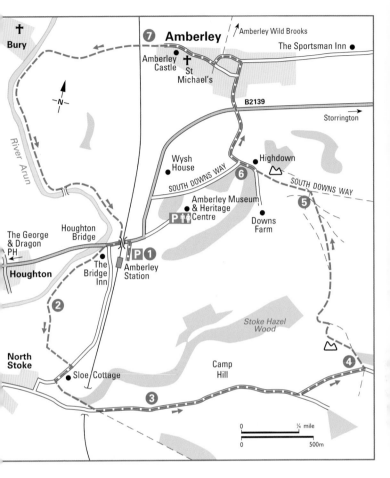

1. Turn left out of the car park and pass underneath the railway bridge. Begin to cross the road bridge spanning the Arun, bearing left at the footpath sign to reach a stile by a galvanised gate. After crossing a bridge and another stile, bear right on a riverside bank to the next stile. A few paces beyond this, reach a sluice. Bear left here.

2. Follow the path between trees, turn right on reaching a lane and pass Sloe Cottage. Turn left just beyond a caravan site to join a bridleway. Follow the path as it runs above the camping ground and emerge on a track by a bridleway sign. Cross the track here and join a rough lane, turning left.

3. Stay on the lane as it climbs gradually; the Arun can be seen below. Pass farm outbuildings and keep ahead, the lane dwindling to a track along this stretch. Veer left at the fork and follow the waymarked public right of way. Head for a signposted crossroads and turn left on a bridleway with a fence on your right.

4. Walk down the flint track, pass through a gate and continue the steep descent. Look for two gates down below, set some distance apart. Cross to the right-hand gate; a bridleway sign should be nearby. Follow the bridleway as it

bends left, climbing steeply towards Downs Farm. Keep a fence on the left and follow the bridleway, eventually merging with a wide track.

5. Keep left at the next junction and follow the South Downs Way towards the entrance to Downs Farm. Fork right at a junction, continuing on the South Downs Way, and join a narrow footpath which begins a steep descent. Drop down the slope until you reach a tarmac lane, then turn right. On the right-hand side is a prominent house called Highdown.

6. Veer right at the fork and walk down to the B2139. Cross over the road into Amberley village and keep ahead at the junction in the village centre. Turn left when you reach a large cottage called The White House and continue to the next road junction with a footpath opposite. Turn right, passing St Michael's Church and Amberley Castle. Carry straight on. Over to the right are glimpses of Amberley Wild Brooks. Where the road ends beneath the castle wall, keep straight ahead on a path between fences.

7. Cross two stiles, either side of the railway, and look for the spire of Bury church ahead. Follow the path to the next stile and cut across the field half left towards a footpath sign and a stile. In the second field make for a stile and bridge ahead, cross the third field in the direction signposted to the riverbank, and turn left. Follow the reed-fringed Arun. Avoid the distinctive metal foot-bridge and keep ahead with the river on the right to return to Houghton Bridge. Bear left for the museum car park.

Where to eat and drink
The Bridge Inn at Houghton Bridge, close to the start of the walk, is Grade II listed and has fires and a welcoming atmosphere. Among the popular dishes are rump steak, steak-and-ale pie, along with ploughman's and sandwiches; also Sunday roasts and a gluten-free menu. There is also a tea room at Houghton Bridge.

What to see
Visit Amberley Wild Brooks, an extensive area of water-meadows. These meadows have been designated a Site of Special Scientific Interest (SSSI) for their diverse habitats – woodland, scrub and dry pasture among them. You may spot Bewick swans and, if you're lucky, white-fronted geese. This is a popular haunt of wintering wildfowl.

While you're there
Take in Amberley Castle, a fortress that dates back to Norman times and was strongly fortified in 1377. Originally it was the residence of the Bishops of Chichester. However, its fate was sealed when the Parliamentarians began to dismantle it during the Civil War. Parts of the castle survive today, having been converted into a stylish hotel. The portcullis closes at midnight every night. A short distance away is the village of Houghton, which you might care to visit after the walk. The George and Dragon pub originally dates back to the 13th century; Charles II stopped here to take ale in October 1651, on his way to the coast after the Battle of Worcester.

EBERNOE COMMON

DISTANCE/TIME	3.5 miles (5.7km) / 1hr 45min
ASCENT/GRADIENT	56ft (17m) / ▲
PATHS	Woodland paths and tracks, field paths and tracks
LANDSCAPE	Heath and wood and former iron industry hammer ponds
SUGGESTED MAP	AA Walker's Map 23 Guildford, Farnham & The Downs
START/FINISH	Grid reference: SU975278
DOG FRIENDLINESS	Cattle have been introduced to graze part of the common
PARKING	Car park by Ebernoe parish church
PUBLIC TOILETS	None on route

In 1980 the Sussex Wildlife Trust bought 185 acres (75ha) of Ebernoe Common, where woodland was under threat. It now owns more, much of which is a Site of Special Scientific Interest (SSSI).

The Trust has a very carefully thought-out management plan to return the common back to wood pasture and restore the glades that were once so characteristic. Wood pasture was a medieval and later use of commons and heaths, where livestock grazed amongst timber trees or 'standards'. Grazing prevented undergrowth and scrub from invading the grassland.

Here you can see ancient oaks and beech trees dotted around, clearings, coppicing and much more besides. Ebernoe Common is rich in species with, for example, more than 900 types of fungi and 375 species of wild flowers and grasses. Sussex cattle have been introduced to restore the character of the common, by grazing away the coarse undergrowth of past neglect.

By the 14th century the common was used for pigs, which fed on acorns and beech nuts. It was also an important source of timber and firewood. In the late 16th century, industry arrived with an iron furnace. A water wheel drove the furnace bellows and trip hammer, powered by water from Furnace Pond. The pond was created by damming a stream, which can be seen on the walk.

The church on the common

The route passes a brick kiln that has recently been restored as part of the common's improvement programme. First shown on an estate map in 1764, the kiln functioned until the 1930s, and made the bricks for Ebernoe church in the 1860s. The Victorian church is built in red brick with bands of yellow and black, a style known as 'constructional polychromy'. Inside, by contrast, it's whitewashed and simple. The lord of the manor, W R Peachey, paid the £1200 building costs, and the churchyard wall was built in brick mainly to keep out the common's rabbits.

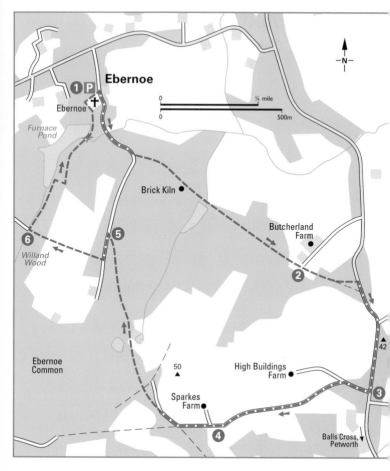

1. From the car park head down the track to the left of the churchyard and a Sussex Wildlife Trust sign. Continue along the track, passing through a gate beside a cattle grid to continue ahead (not right), through old hazel coppicing amid the oak, beech and ash trees. You pass a brick kiln, a Scheduled Ancient Monument, and cross a causeway past a pond. The path ascends again. At a fork bear left. The ground levels and continues to a gate by another cattle grid. Through this continue on the path, and where a grassy area appears on the right, enter it to emerge from the wooded common.

2. Continue across the grass, a farmhouse with a large pond in its garden to your left. Go along the edge of the woods, on a wide grass strip. Where the hedge goes left continue ahead into the wood and wind through the wood. Bear right along a lane.

3. Turn right on a farm road by a footpath sign, then take the first fork left, signed to Sparkes Farm. Continue along this track between trim hedges, diverting at a kissing gate to read about the Butcherland Fields restoration project on an information board. Back on the track, continue to the crest.

4. Continue past Sparkes Farm to your right, and follow the track through a gate. After 50yds (46m), ignore a path signposted to the left, carry on along the track for another 150yds (137m), then fork left at the signpost with a nature reserve sign into the wooded common at a footpath post. Follow the path and bear half right at a footpath post and cross a footbridge. Continue to another footbridge between ponds. Pass through a bridlegate and follow the clear path.

5. Pass between three posts and bear left along a track as far as a footpath sign where you bear right along a track to a bridle gate. Through the gate, you cross a field alongside a hedge. From the field corner descend into Willand Wood.

6. Just before two streams (with a footbridge crossing the further one) bear right and follow the winding path roughly parallel to a stream. The path climbs right and continues to the banks of a large hammer pond, Furnace Pond. Cross the footbridge over the outlet weir and bear left, still alongside the pond, and climb steps out of the valley. At the top bear half right to the church.

Where to eat and drink
Carry on along the lane from waypoint 3 for 500yds (457m) to Balls Cross and the Stag Inn. It is well known for its stone flagged floors and traditional country food, including game in season.

What to see
In autumn the bright red caps of the fly agaric toadstool dot the common, eventually dying off into blackened ruin. Their caps start off dome-shaped, and later flatten and are dotted with white, warty spots. Although pretty, this toadstool is highly toxic.

While you're there
If you are walking with young children, you could head a few miles east, passing through Kirdford to Wisborough Green. At Fishers Farm Park children can enjoy farm rides, an enchanted wood and play castle, and meet the farm animals.

AROUND PETWORTH

DISTANCE/TIME	3.5 miles (5.7km) / 1hr 45min
ASCENT/GRADIENT	205ft (63m) / ▲
PATHS	Field paths and tracks, pavements in Petworth, several stiles
LANDSCAPE	Rolling, pastoral countryside, woodland and a historic townscape
SUGGESTED MAP	OS Explorer OL33 Haslemere & Petersfield
START/FINISH	Grid reference: SU976215
DOG FRIENDLINESS	On a lead through the horse and cattle pasture on the northern section of the walk and on lead in town
PARKING	Car park in the centre of Petworth
PUBLIC TOILETS	In the car park

Petworth town perches, precariously hemmed in between the walls of Petworth House's grounds and the deep-cut valley that lies to the east of the town. Its streets are narrow with sharp corners, and it has always been a traffic bottleneck. In the 1970s Petworth was threatened with a north–south bypass. The problem was its route. If it went west it would destroy much of Petworth House's superb great park, designed by 'Capability' Brown and painted by William Turner. If it went east the road would destroy the delightful countryside through which this walk passes. Either route would be potentially disastrous to the surroundings of this historic town. A vigorous campaign succeeded in stopping the bypass, but of course the traffic has not gone away.

Lombard Street is the prettiest in the town, and traffic free, while East Street has the grandest town houses. The area around the market square has many timber-framed buildings, and the town is full of antique shops. In the centre is the 1793 town hall, a two-storey stone building with arched windows.

An unexpected pleasure of Petworth are the numerous estate workers' buildings, all painted in the same shade of maroon, tucked around back streets. In the High Street at the end of the walk, you pass the tiny Petworth Cottage Museum (open most afternoons, April to October), in the former home of Mrs Mary Cummings, employed as a seamstress. It is evocatively furnished as it might have looked when she lived there around 1910.

Petworth church tower is a curious structure. Stone in the lower stages, the upper part is brick, added in 1827. It was originally rendered, and above it was a spire more suited to a suburban church in Ealing. Apparently Sir Charles Barry employed a design he was preparing for a church in Brighton. The spire was removed in 1947, and the present parapet and shallow tiled pyramidal roof built in 1953.

The walk passes through Byworth, a small village poised above the east bank of the deep-cut stream. Apart from an old pub, The Black Horse, there are two very attractive and much photographed and painted cottages where the route turns left off the main street. Both have whitewashed infill panels to their timber framing and are jettied, the upper storey projecting on curved brackets beyond the ground floor.

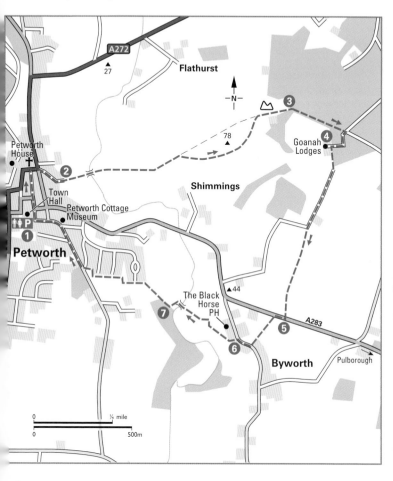

1. Leave the car park via the Old Bakery Shopping Arcade and its thriving independent bookshop. Continue up towards the distant church tower. Pass the Town Hall and continue up Lombard Street. At the top bear right towards Sir Charles Barry's 1851 Gothic lamp standard and cross East Street into Bartons Lane (seen to the left). Follow this downhill, as it becomes a footpath.

2. Go through a kissing gate where there is a splendid view across the valley and a rolling pastoral landscape, unbelievably, once threatened with a bypass. Go through a second kissing gate and, ignoring paths to the left and right, descend to a stone bridge, then over it, continuing ahead to a hedge corner. Reaching this, continue ahead alongside the hedge. Through a kissing gate

with the Serpent Trail waymarker, carry on up, then at the crest go forward just to the right of the nearest clump of pines.

3. Descend to a kissing gate by an oak tree and, once through this, ascend between hedges. At a junction at the top bear half right and continue on the track along the edge of and then within woodland. Continue ahead over two cross tracks, and where the path meets a metalled track bear sharp right along it towards a pair of large stone Petworth Estate gate piers beside the Goanah Lodges.

4. Just before the gate piers turn left onto a track passing a covered reservoir, and follow this out of the woods. Descend past farm buildings and where the track bends right go forward on an unmarked path that is all but swallowed by bracken in summer. Cross a large field, past the nearest tree and maintain the same direction.

5. Emerge by a narrow gap in the hedge onto the road, turn right along it and immediately left over a stile. Over this follow a fence to the bottom far corner of the field and drop to a gate and stile, followed quickly by another gate. Through this turn right on the lane through Byworth village.

6. Go left at a telephone box by a house with a Hovis sign, onto a tarmac lane, then through a gate ahead. Follow a path that bears right to a footbridge, a pond to your left, and cross a stile. Now in a paddock, go left alongside a fence and at the end climb a stile and bear left down to a footbridge over a stream.

7. Over the footbridge bear right and climb, continuing through a kissing gate. After a few paces bear left at an unwaymarked path fork and climb a field towards houses. At the crest keep ahead on a path between fences, garden fences and hedges to your right. Reaching the road bear right and follow it. The road eventually curves left and becomes the High Street on its way into the town centre. Go past the Petworth Cottage Museum and at the T-junction bear left back to the car park.

Where to eat and drink

If you continue further along Byworth's main street, The Black Horse is an excellent country pub with a restaurant. In Petworth there is plenty of choice, including the Hungry Guest Café in Lombard Street.

What to see

Look to the sky and you may see a red kite soaring above you. This beautiful bird is spreading inland from the South Downs. Reintroduced into the Chiltern Hills from Spain and Scandinavia in 1989 by the RSPB and the Nature Conservancy Council, this has been an extraordinarily successful project.

While you're there

Petworth House, behind its wall, backs onto the town in an unusually intimate way for England. French 17th- and 18th-century architects have been named as possible designers. Besides the National Trust-owned mansion there are 700 acres (283ha) of deer park to explore.

AROUND BIGNOR'S ROMAN REMAINS

DISTANCE/TIME	5.25 miles (8.5km) / 2hrs
ASCENT/GRADIENT	773ft (236m) / ▲ ▲
PATHS	Downland and woodland tracks and paths, country roads
LANDSCAPE	Rolling countryside and well-wooded slopes
SUGGESTED MAP	AA Walker's Map 20 Chichester & The South Downs
START/FINISH	Grid reference: SU974129
DOG FRIENDLINESS	Quiet lanes with little traffic. Parts of walk follow tracks and paths where dogs can run free. No dogs on villa grounds
PARKING	Bignor Hill free car park
PUBLIC TOILETS	Bignor Villa – open March to October
NOTES	Before setting off on this walk it's worth walking up to the top of nearby Bignor Hill (c.1 mile/1.6km there and back) for the views

Bignor is most famous for its Roman villa situated just outside the village, a vineyard planted on the slopes below. From here the eye is drawn south towards the northern escarpment of the South Downs and Bignor Hill, which rises to 738ft (225m). From this lofty vantage point there are excellent views east along the length of the Downs towards the Arun Valley and beyond. In spring and summer the grassland is full of wild flowers and butterflies.

Bignor Hill is part of the National Trust's 1,400 hectare Slindon Estate. About 1 mile (1.6km) southwest of its car park is Gumber Farm, also part of the estate, which has an interesting history. During World War II it was used as a decoy airfield, using lights at night and wooden aeroplanes during the day to mimic a military airfield, and thus attempt to protect the real airfields at Ford and Tangmere from being bombed. Today it is a working sheep farm and has a camping barn and field.

The Roman Villa at Bignor is one of the largest in Britain. Discovered by a ploughman in 1811, Bignor features various mosaics which are considered to be among the finest in the country, depicting scenes of gladiators and representations of Venus and Medusa. Originally the villa consisted of about 70 buildings situated in a walled enclosure of over 4 acres (1.6ha). The estate may have extended to about 200 acres (81ha), confirming that a wealthy or influential person would have lived here, possibly the equivalent of a modern aristocrat. Construction of the building probably started around the end of the 2nd century AD and it may have been occupied for at least 200 years.

The Grade I listed Holy Cross Church in Bignor largely dates to the 13th century, though a notable feature to be seen here is the 11th-century Norman arch dividing the nave and chancel. The font is also Norman. The church is used on a regular basis for concerts, talks, poetry readings, art exhibitions and festivals.

Dating from 1420 and Grade II listed, the Yeoman's House is a superb example of a medieval hall house, today available for holiday letting. This walk starts high, takes you down to Bignor with a chance to visit the Roman villa, before climbing back up again to the top. The views are well worth the effort.

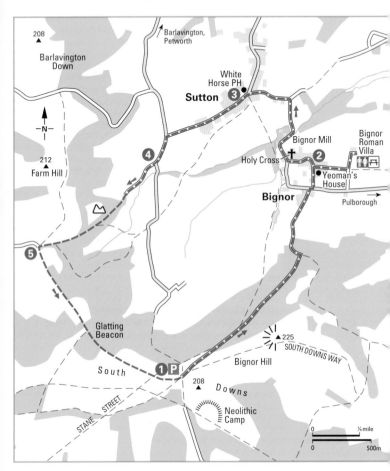

1. From the car park, where there's a large wooden signpost and information board, follow the tarmac lane down towards Bignor Roman Villa. The lane descends through the woodland, passing a bridleway on the right as it bends left. On reaching Bignor village, pass a farm and bear briefly right and then left to take the road ahead, signposted 'Sutton and Duncton'. Pass a telephone box, and on the right is the picturesque Yeoman's House. To visit the Roman villa, turn right along the access road here, continuing along a footpath. On reaching the drive turn left to the entrance.

2. Retrace your steps to the Yeoman's House and bear right along the road. The road bends left and passes the Parish Church of Holy Cross. A yew tree, so

familiar to country churchyards, can be seen in the corner. Follow the lane, ignoring a left turn, as it descends steeply through the trees and then climbs between high hedges towards Sutton. Pass the village sign and follow the road as it bends left by a bridleway running off to the right. Walk into the village.

3. When the road bends right by the White Horse, go straight on towards Barlavington and Duncton. Follow the lane between stone-built houses and cottages and head out of the village. Keep left at the fork and follow the 'No through road'. A tree-clad scarp, the walk's next objective, looms ahead.

4. As the lane bends left, fork right on the bridleway. Further on, the track can become wet and muddy underfoot at the point where you share the route with a stream. Begin a gentle, slow ascent through the woodland and gradually the path narrows and becomes progressively steeper. At a fork, keep left. The dramatic ascent eases further up and here you avoid a left-hand footpath. Soon daylight can be seen ahead, reaching through the trees.

5. At a meeting point of tracks, go forward and then bear left after about 30yds (27m). Follow the chalk track as it climbs gently, with far-ranging views over remote, well-wooded country. The track curves towards two masts on Glatting Beacon, peeping above the trees. Pass a National Trust sign for Bignor Hill and a bridleway on the right. Keep forward through woodland and now the track begins a gentle descent. Gradually the views widen to reveal glorious woodland and downland stretching into the distance. Head down to a junction, keep ahead on the South Downs Way and follow it back to the car park.

Where to eat and drink
Bignor Roman Villa includes a free picnic area for visitors and tea rooms providing tea, coffee and light snacks. The newly refurbished White Horse pub at Sutton lies at the foot of the South Downs, directly on the walk. There is a good choice of food and a selection of popular beers.

What to see
Near the end of the walk is a charming dew pond, one of a number to be found on the South Downs. Originally used for watering sheep before there was piped water and troughs, these traditional ponds are important wildlife habitats as well as a classic feature of the landscape. Dew ponds really owe their name to folklore. The vast majority of the water that fills them comes from rainfall.

While you're there
Pause to appreciate the landscape and history of the South Downs near Bignor. There is strong evidence of the Roman occupation here and running across Bignor Hill is Stane Street, a Roman road constructed about AD 70 to connect the port of Chichester (Noviomagus) with London (Londinium), a distance of some 56 miles (90km). The National Trust owns several miles of it. You pass a section of the road at the end of the walk when you join the South Downs Way. The raised bank ('agger') you see marks the route of the old road. Today a stretch of the Monarch's Way follows it southwest.

EXPLORING THE SLINDON ESTATE

41

DISTANCE/TIME	5.5 miles (8.9km) / 3hrs
ASCENT/GRADIENT	570ft (174m) / ▲ ▲
PATHS	Woodland, downland paths and tracks
LANDSCAPE	Sweeping downland and woodland
SUGGESTED MAP	AA Walker's Map 20 Chichester & The South Downs
START/FINISH	Grid reference: SU960076
DOG FRIENDLINESS	Dogs under close control on Slindon Estate and in Slindon village
PARKING	Free National Trust car park in Park Lane, Slindon
PUBLIC TOILETS	None on route

It all began in 1895, the year the National Trust was founded by three visionary Victorians whose objective was to acquire sites of historic interest and natural beauty for the benefit of the nation. More than 120 years after its foundation, it is now the country's biggest landowner, depending on donations and legacies and the annual subscriptions of its two million members for much of its income. Over the years it has acquired 610,000 acres (247,000ha) of countryside, much of which is freely open to everyone, 775 miles (1,247km) of coastline, over 500 historic buildings and more than 200 gardens, all of which it aims to preserve and protect for future generations. It is some achievement.

Much of the West Sussex village of Slindon is part of the National Trust's 3,500-acre (1,419ha) Slindon Estate, which is situated on the southern slopes of the South Downs between Arundel and Chichester. The estate was originally designed and developed as an integrated community and the Trust aims to maintain this structure as far as possible. Take a stroll through Slindon village as you end the walk and you can see that many of the cottages are built of brick and flint, materials typical of chalk country. During the medieval period, long before the National Trust was established, Slindon was an important estate of the Archbishops of Canterbury. Even earlier than this it was home to Neolithic people who settled at Barkhale, a hilltop site at its northern end.

As well as the village, the estate consists of a large expanse of sweeping downland dissected by dry valleys, a folly, several farms and a stretch of Roman road. Parts of the estate were damaged in the storms of 1987 and 1990, though the woods are regenerating. Typical ground plants include bluebell, dog's mercury, greater butterfly orchid and wood sedge.

To help celebrate its centenary in 1995, the National Trust chose the Slindon Estate to launch its 100 Paths Project, a scheme designed to enhance access to its countryside properties by creating or improving paths. This glorious, unspoiled landscape offers many miles of footpaths and bridleways, making it an excellent choice for a country walk.

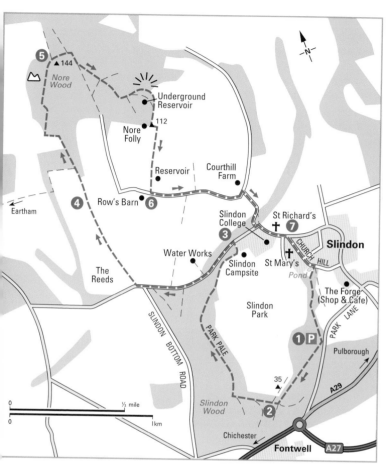

1. From the car park walk towards the road and turn right, passing through the gate to join a wide straight path cutting between trees and bracken. The path runs alongside sunny glades and clearings and between lines of attractive beech and silver birch trees before reaching a crossroads.

2. Turn right to a second crossroads and continue ahead here, keeping the grassy bank and ditch (all that remains of the Park Pale), on your right. Follow the broad path as it begins a wide curve around to the right. The boundary ditch is still visible here, running parallel to the path you are on. On reaching a kissing gate, continue ahead, soon skirting fields. As you approach the entrance to Slindon campsite, swing left and follow the track down to the road.

3. Turn left and follow the road through the woodland. Pass Slindon Bottom Road and turn right after a few paces to join a bridleway. Follow the path as it cuts between fields.

4. Ignore a footpath to the left signed 'Eartham ¾m' and continue forwards. The ascent becoming slightly steeper as the path twists and turns through the wood.

145

5. Eventually the path curves to the right to round the summit of Nore Hill and begins to descend gently at a guidepost. Turn right at a T-junction shortly afterwards and then bear left at a fork past a barrier and along a straight track. This eventually turns sharp left and swings right to leave the woods and provide glorious views of the estate. Pass Nore Folly on your right and follow the track as it turns left and right and begins to descend.

6. Continue straight ahead along the track, following it gently down. Pass Courthill Farm on the left and turn right at the road. Follow the lane, or soon branch left on to a parallel woodland path to the next road. Bear left and pass Slindon College on the right and St Richard's Catholic Church on the left before reaching Church Hill.

7. Fork right into Church Hill, pass the church and make for the pond, a familiar weeping willow reaching down to the water's edge. Look for mallard ducks here. Turn right around the far end of the pond on the obvious waterside path to enter the wood. On reaching a fork, by a National Trust sign for the Slindon Estate, keep left and walk ahead through the trees, ignoring any side paths, to return to the car park.

Where to eat and drink

The George at Eartham (off the route by 0.75 miles/1.2km) serves traditional pub food as well as seasonal dishes using local produce. The bar and dining room are open-plan and there is a secluded beer garden. The historic old village forge at Slindon has a shop and café, offering light lunches and afternoon teas.

What to see

As you stroll through peaceful Slindon Wood look for the remains of the medieval Park Pale, more commonly described as a bank and ditch. This was originally designed to protect the park's deer. In Palaeolithic times, the sea extended this far inland – hard to believe now as you look at the wooded surroundings. A preserved shingle beach indicates that the sea was once 130ft (40m) higher than it is today. Courthill Farm, towards the end of the walk, was once the home of the French-born writer Hilaire Belloc and his wife when they were first married. He spent part of his childhood in the village.

While you're there

Have a look at the church of St Mary, partly Norman and greatly restored. Inside is a rare wooden effigy to Sir Anthony St Leger, a Tudor politician, who died in 1539. Slindon House, now part of a college, was one of the rest-houses of the Archbishops of Canterbury during the Middle Ages.

TENNYSON'S BLACK DOWN

DISTANCE/TIME	6 miles (9.7km) / 3hrs
ASCENT/GRADIENT	480ft (146m) / ▲ ▲
PATHS	Woodland paths and tracks, farmland and some minor roads
LANDSCAPE	Wooded hills on Sussex/Surrey Border
SUGGESTED MAP	AA Walker's Map 23 Guildford, Farnham & The Downs
START/FINISH	Grid reference: SU922306
DOG FRIENDLINESS	Off lead away from car park and roads
PARKING	Free car park off Tennyson's Lane (by National Trust sign for Blackdown), near Aldworth House to the southeast of Haslemere
PUBLIC TOILETS	None on route

Black Down lies in some of the loveliest countryside in southern England. At 919ft (280m), this prominent, pine-clad summit is the highest point in the county, yet for some reason it has never achieved the popular status of other high Sussex landmarks such as Devil's Dyke, Ditchling Beacon or Ashdown Forest. Part of a plateau of nearly 500 acres (202ha), Black Down is owned and cared for by the National Trust.

The Victorians made it a popular local destination for walkers and naturalists. One man in particular gave Black Down his personal stamp of approval – Alfred, Lord Tennyson. The Poet Laureate built his second home here in 1868, living at Aldworth House for the last 24 years of his life. Tennyson was greatly inspired by the beauty and solitude of the area.

Black Down is part of the range of sandstone hills which is enclosed by the bowl-shaped perimeter of the North and South Downs. Historic artefacts found in this area indicate that there was human activity here as early as the middle Stone Age, 6000 BC. Although the area has been referred to as southeast England's 'Black Country', Black Down's name comes from the firs which rise out of a dark, heathery landscape, and not from the iron industry which once flourished around here. Some of the most ancient tracks in Sussex cut across this hill, and the area was once a haunt of smugglers who may have used a cave here to hide their contraband, en route to London from the south coast.

Not surprisingly, Black Down was chosen as a beacon site, one of a chain to warn London of the threat of invasion on the south coast. The coming of the Spanish Armada in July 1588 was relayed via the beacon here, which would have been lit on a position high up, overlooking the Sussex Weald.

This superb walk explores Black Down and its hidden corners. Not only does it guide you to one of the loveliest viewpoints in Sussex, but it allows you to picture its most distinguished resident, Alfred, Lord Tennyson, strolling this glorious plateau and savouring its views.

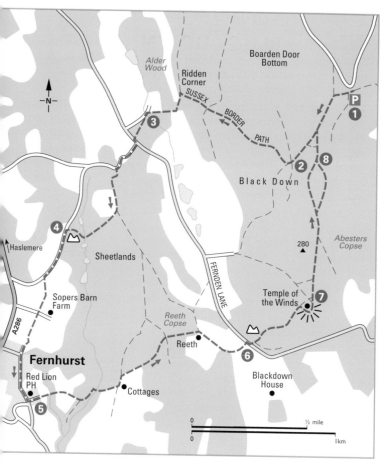

1. Turn left out of the car park and immediately left again on a rising path to the right of the National Trust sign. Keep left at the junction, then bear right at the fork and keep right just before a pond, also right, on the Sussex Border Path and Serpent Trail.

2. Take the second right at a junction of paths. Keep left at the fork, still on the Sussex Border Path, and pass over a crossroads and through a gate. Veer left just beyond it at the fork and drop down to some rhododendron bushes. Turn sharp left here through a gate and follow the path through a tunnel of trees.

3. Bear left at a drive by a house and when, after a few paces, it curves right, go straight on to the right of a pond through the trees to join the road. Turn left and then immediately right at the sign for Sheetlands. Follow the tarmac drive through the trees down to a bridleway sign. Go left up the bank, veering right at the top, and keep to the path as it runs above the drive. Pass above houses and turn right, just after a thatched house, by a waymarker post. Passing some Gothic wooden gates in a hedge to your right, descend an enclosed path, which bends left at the bottom and immediately right by a pond and climbs quite steeply.

149

4. Turn left at a signposted T-junction and then, ignoring a track to the left, follow the driveway past an ornate lamp standard. After 150m, turn left on a signposted path, along a line of trees and over stiles. Cross over a driveway and take the path opposite, heading towards Fernhurst. Join a tarmac drive, turn left at the road and then walk through the village to the Red Lion, overlooking the spacious green.

5. On leaving the inn, turn immediately left and follow the tarmac drive, which soon becomes a woodland track. Ignore a track off to the left and later bear left then right over a stream. Turn left by a wooden barn and cottages and veer right at the next waymarked fork. Now begin a moderate and perennially muddy ascent through the trees. Cross a wide track and continue the climb up through the woodland. Keep right by a house called Reeth. The track bends round to the left and runs up to a junction with a minor road.

6. Make for a signposted bridleway on the left. After a few paces reach a National Trust sign. Keep left here and follow the sunken path as it climbs between trees, steeply in places. On the higher ground, follow the path as it winds pleasantly between bracken and silver birch. Fork right past a seat which takes advantage of a magnificent view, partly obscured by trees. Veer right, keeping the seat and the view on your right and walk along the level to the curved stone seat at what is known as the Temple of the Winds.

7. Take the path running up behind the seat, very soon keeping right and right again. Keep ahead past a path running off sharp right and then a flight of steps, and veer left or right at the next signposted fork: both paths merge.

8. Continue ahead and veer right at the next fork. Keep ahead at the next junction, now following part of the Sussex Border Path again and retracing your initial outward steps. Veer to the right at the fork, still following the long-distance trail, and head back down the road to the entrance to the car park.

Where to eat and drink
The Red Lion at Fernhurst overlooks the village green. On warm summer days, there's nothing to beat sitting outside this 500-year-old building and enjoying its setting. There's a good range of beers and a varied menu. Bar meals are served all week and the restaurant is open every day.

What to see
Black Down's plateau was once an extensive heath managed as common pasture with bracken cut and gathered for bedding. Thousands of years of grazing sustained our heathlands, but since 1950 nearly half of it has been lost. Before grazing stopped, much of the site consisted of gorse and heathland plant. Later, Scots pine, birch and rhododendron began to grow. The main summit area is dominated by heather, with wetland plants. Pine woodland is prolific here, with rowan, birch, gorse, bramble and bilberry. Birds include nuthatch, woodcock, nightjar, linnet and yellowhammer.

While you're there
The views from the Temple of the Winds are outstanding. Tennyson's old summerhouse stood near the memorial seat here.

MEANDERING AROUND MIDHURST

DISTANCE/TIME	3 miles (4.8km) / 2hrs
ASCENT/GRADIENT	123ft (37m) / ▲
PATHS	Pavements, field, riverside tracks and country road
LANDSCAPE	Midhurst town and its beautiful rural setting on the Rother
SUGGESTED MAP	AA Walker's Map 20 Chichester & The South Downs
START/FINISH	Grid reference: SU887217
DOG FRIENDLINESS	Off lead on tracks and stretches of riverside. On lead on roads and busy streets in Midhurst town centre
PARKING	Car park at north end of town in North Street
PUBLIC TOILETS	Car park

Midhurst is one of those classic Sussex towns crying out to be discovered and explored on foot, with many splendid buildings and a wealth of history. H G Wells attended school at Midhurst and wrote: 'I found something very agreeable and picturesque in its clean and cobbled streets, its odd turnings and abrupt corners, and in the pleasant park that crowds up one side of the town.' Midhurst became the model for Wimblehurst in his book *Tono-Bungay*.

Look around you on this walk and you'll spot the vivid yellow paintwork of houses owned by the Cowdray Estate. The grounds of Cowdray Park are famous for polo matches. Not so well known are the majestic ruins of Cowdray House, seen from the car park at the start of the walk and viewed up close just before you finish it. The house, built for the Earl of Southampton, dates back to about 1530 but was largely destroyed by fire in 1793. However, the shell survives and, if open, you can see around the Great Chamber, the Great Parlour and the Chapel.

Begin the walk by embarking on a town trail. Old photographs of the town taken in the early part of the 20th century show the part-16th-century Angel Hotel and the building which now houses Barclays Bank. The famous tile-hung library has been preserved too, and the medieval interior is certainly worth looking at. Built in the early part of the 16th century, the building was thought originally to have been a storehouse or granary. This part of Midhurst is known as Knockhundred Row. The delightfully evocative name is thought to date back to the time when Midhurst had a castle, and the owner could exercise his right to summon 100 men to defend the castle by knocking on the doors of 100 households in the town. The road passes the old chemist shop where HG Wells worked before attending Midhurst Grammar School. His mother was housekeeper at nearby Uppark House. In the middle of the street, flanked by striking houses and shop fronts, lies the town's war memorial on which the names of several regiments are recorded. Follow the road to the church of St Mary Magdalene and St Denys. The walk, ideal for a summer's evening, eventually leaves Midhurst and heads for rolling, wooded countryside. But it's not long before you are returning to the town, following a path running through woodland above the Rother. Here you can step between the trees on the right to look down at the river and across to Cowdray House. This vista is one of the highlights of the walk, a moment to savour on the homeward leg. The walk finishes by following the Queen's Path, a favourite walk of Elizabeth I.

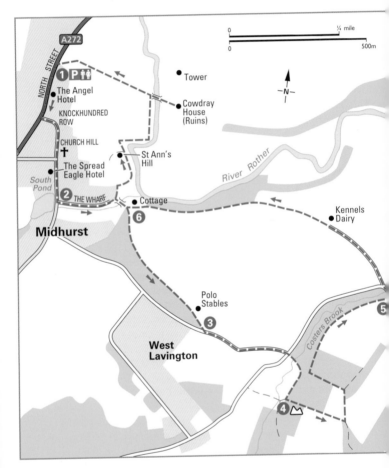

1. From the car park at the north end of the town turn left and walk along North Street, passing The Angel Hotel. Bear left into Knockhundred Row; the road bends right and becomes Church Hill. When it splits (one-way traffic) keep left, passing the war memorial on your right and the church on your left. Continue into South Street past the historic Spread Eagle Hotel.

2. Turn left by South Pond into The Wharf, keeping right along the road beside industrial buildings and flats. Turn right to cross a river bridge and pass a cottage on the left. Keep the wooden fencing on the right and avoid the path

running off to the left. Go through a kissing gate, then continue ahead along the edge of fields, keeping trees and vegetation on the right. Go through another kissing gate and follow the path to the right of the polo stables. Come armed with a stick to beat back the nettles that devour this path in summer.

3. Keep left and follow a pleasantly wooded stretch of road. Pass some pretty cottages, and on reaching a bend keep ahead along a bridle path signposted 'Heyshott and Graffham'. Follow the track as it curves to the right.

4. Veer left at a fingerpost just before the entrance to a house and follow the waymarked path as it climbs quite steeply through the trees, passing between woodland glades and carpets of bracken. Drop down the slope to a junction and turn left along a sandy track. Keep left at the fork and follow the track as it bends sharply to the right.

5. On reaching the road, turn left and, when it bends left by some gates, go straight on along the bridleway towards Kennels Dairy. Pass between two rows of stables and carry on ahead. Continue on the path and, when it reaches a field gateway, go through the gate to the right of it, following the path as it runs just inside the woodland.

6. Continue along to the junction, forming part of the outward leg of the walk, turn right and cross the bridge. Keep ahead past the access road/bridleway on the left (your outward route), then bear right to rejoin the riverbank. Keep going until you reach a footpath on the left leading up to the ruins of St Ann's Hill. Follow the path beside the Rother, curving right. Continue to a kissing gate, bear left and carry on to a bridge which provides access to Cowdray House, where there is free entrance to a walled garden and tea rooms. After viewing the house, go straight ahead along the causeway path to the car park.

Where to eat and drink
Midhurst has several pubs and hotels, among them The Angel Hotel in North Street. This extended Tudor coaching inn has a restaurant, set lunches through the week and light snacks in the more informal surroundings of the bar. Cockburn's Tea Rooms, behind Midhurst Museum in Knockhundred Row, and the Olive & Vine in North Street offer tea, coffee and lunches.

What to see
South Pond is one of Midhurst's most popular attractions. Donated to the town by Lord Cowdray in 1957, the pond is part of a tributary of the Rother. Mute swans, Canada geese and mallards can be seen here. A path running alongside South Pond was opened in 1977 to mark the Queen's Silver Jubilee.

While you're there
Have a look at St Ann's Hill, just off the route of the walk, above the River Rother. This natural mound was once the site of a fortified Norman castle, though all that remains of it today are a few stones amid this grassy knoll.

A GLORIOUS GOODWOOD LOOP

DISTANCE/TIME	5 miles (8km) / 2hr 15min
ASCENT/GRADIENT	385ft (117m) / ▲
PATHS	Woodland tracks and field paths, section of Monarch's Way and one lengthy stretch of quiet road, several stiles
LANDSCAPE	Mixture of dense woodland and scenic downland
SUGGESTED MAP	AA Walker's Map 20 Chichester & The South Downs
START/FINISH	Grid reference: SU898113
DOG FRIENDLINESS	Off lead on woodland tracks
PARKING	Counter's Gate free car park and picnic area at Goodwood Country Park
PUBLIC TOILETS	Weald and Downland Living Museum

Think of horse racing on the South Downs and you immediately think of Goodwood, without doubt one of Britain's loveliest and most famous racecourses. The course rises and falls around a natural amphitheatre, with the horses dashing along the ridge to create one of the greatest spectacles in the racing world. Its superb position amid magnificent beechwoods high on the Downs draws crowds from far and wide, and for one week every summer it becomes 'Glorious Goodwood', when thousands of racegoers travel to Sussex to attend one of the most prestigious events of the sporting and social calendar. According to *The Times*, Goodwood is 'the place to be and to be seen'.

The course opened in 1801 after the Duke of Richmond gave part of his estate, Goodwood Park, to establish a track where members of the Goodwood Hunt Club and officers of the Sussex Militia could attend meetings. However, Goodwood's track record has not always been unblemished. Towards the end of the 19th century the racecourse acquired a rather unfortunate reputation in the area when the rector of nearby Singleton protested to the Chief Constable in the strongest terms over the rowdy behaviour of racegoers. As a result, the crowds were restrained.

The walk begins at Goodwood Country Park, a popular amenity area characterised by woodland and downland grass, and initially follows part of the Monarch's Way through extensive woodland and down to the village of East Dean. Along the road is neighbouring Charlton, most famous for the Charlton Hunt. Established in the 18th century, perhaps the hunt's most memorable chase took place on 28 January 1738, beginning before eight that morning and not finishing until nearly six that evening. Many of those taking part were from the elite, upper ranks of society and for 10 hours that day a fox led the pack a merry dance in the surrounding fields and woods. Eventually, the hounds cornered their prey, an elderly vixen, near the River Arun. It wasn't until 2004 that the barbaric practice was outlawed in Britain.

At this point you should visit the Weald and Downland Living Museum, with its unusual collection of traditional homes and workplaces in both village and countryside. The main walk finishes by skirting Goodwood and on race days crowds line the bridleway alongside it, watching as camera crews dash back and forth in an effort to capture the best television images. The sound of the PA system floats across the course as you witness all the colourful activity.

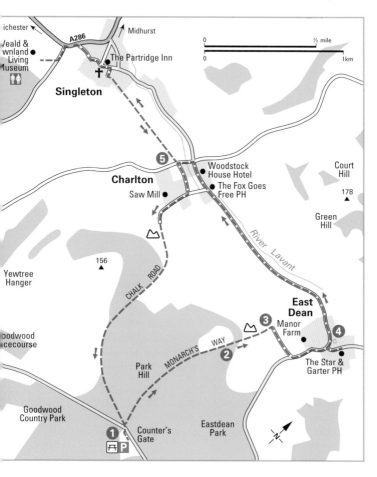

1. Make for the western end of Counter's Gate car park and head out on a footpath that skirts a field, then goes through a copse and bears right onto a road. Cross over (taking great care at this fast blind bend) to a junction of two clear tracks, with a path on the right. Follow the right-hand track, which is signposted 'public footpath' and forms part of the Monarch's Way, to a five-bar gate and stile. Continue along to the next stile and then cross a clearing in the woods until you come to a fingerpost beneath the trees at the far end.

2. Follow the path briefly through the woods to emerge at the top of a field. The village of East Dean can be seen nestling down below. Head diagonally right down the steep field slope to reach a stile in the corner.

3. Cross into the adjacent field and follow the boundary to a second stile leading out to the road. Bear left and walk down into East Dean, passing Manor Farm. Keep right at the junction in the village centre and, if it's opening time, follow the road towards Petworth in order to visit The Star & Garter pub.

4. Leave East Dean by keeping the pond on your right-hand side and follow the road towards Midhurst and Singleton. On reaching Charlton village, pass the Fox Goes Free pub and take the next left turning. Follow the lane to a stile on the right and a turning on the left. Cross over into the fields and follow the straight path. At the end of the field bear right then go through a kissing gate and along an enclosed path to a residential road. Keep straight ahead and then continue along a walkway between houses. You'll reach a green and playground with the church beyond. Turn right from the church car park to the road, left past The Partridge Inn, left at the main road and left again. The Weald and Downland Living Museum at Singleton is just up this road on the right. Return to this stile by the same route and take the road opposite.

5. Walk along to the junction and turn right by the war memorial, dedicated to fallen comrades of the Sussex Yeomanry in both World Wars. Follow the track (Chalky Road) past houses and then on up through the trees. On the left are glimpses of a glorious rolling landscape, while to the right Goodwood's superb downland racecourse edges into view between the trees. Stay on the track all the way to the road and cross over to return to the Counter's Gate car park.

Where to eat and drink

The Star & Garter at East Dean and the 400-year-old The Fox Goes Free at Charlton both offer a good range of meals and snacks and enjoy a pleasant South Downs setting. There is a café at the Weald and Downland Living Museum offering soup, filled rolls, quiche, Cornish pasties, and cakes and pastries made with flour from the local working watermill.

What to see

The village of East Dean, with its pond and ancient cottages of Sussex flint, is one of the prettiest in the area. For many years it was a thriving centre for hurdlemaking, and before World War I seven craftsmen operated here.

While you're there

Visit the Weald and Downland Living Museum, which includes many attractions. Set in 50 acres (20ha) of lovely Sussex countryside, the museum offers a fascinating collection of some 50 regional historic buildings, which have been saved from destruction, painstakingly restored and rebuilt in their original form. You can discover Victorian labourers' cottages, visit a recreated Tudor farmstead and tour the remarkable, prizewinning Downland Gridshell.

DOWNLAND HISTORY AT EAST LAVANT

DISTANCE/TIME	5 miles (8km) / 2hrs
ASCENT/GRADIENT	550ft (168m) / ▲
PATHS	Downland paths, bridleways and tracks. Includes a section of Goodwood Lavant Valley Cycle Route
LANDSCAPE	Open downland and farmland
SUGGESTED MAP	AA Walker's Map 20 Chichester & The South Downs
START/FINISH	Grid reference: SU872110
DOG FRIENDLINESS	Dogs to be kept on lead over all downland in order to safeguard rare ground-nesting birds. Keep under control on village roads and patches of farmland
PARKING	Free parking at Seven Points, Goodwood Country Park (closes at dusk)
PUBLIC TOILETS	None on route

On a fine day, the views from the car park alone at the start of this spectacular walk will lift your spirits. The coastal plain stretches out below you, with Chichester to the south, and beyond to the west the Isle of Wight is clearly visible. But there's even better to come from the top of the nearby Trundle hill-fort, which affords an unforgettable view of the Sussex countryside.

The Trundle, from the Old English word meaning circle, crowns the top of St Roche's Hill – the site, too, of two large radio masts. (They lack in aesthetic value, but they do provide a useful landmark.) The Trundle, made up of a ditch, dyke and banks, stands 675ft (206m) above sea level and began life as a neolithic enclosure. Iron Age people later occupied the site, and during the Middle Ages a chapel stood here. Later still, a windmill crowned the summit, which was adorned with eight masts during World War II.

On the far side of this impressive fortified hilltop, Goodwood Racecourse suddenly looms into view, catching you completely by surprise when you walk up here. The gleaming grandstand and the racecourse's natural amphitheatre setting create a stunning picture. It's a good, free vantage point for viewing the races. It's well worth walking at least part-way round the ramparts to enjoy the views to the full, splendid towards the south coast, but lovely inland too.

Goodwood House, one of the finest stately homes in the country, has been the home of the Dukes of Richmond and Lennox for over 300 years. Situated a couple of miles to the east of the walk, surrounded by mature parklands, it's open to visitors from March to October. As well as the racecourse, Goodwood also has a motor racing circuit – its Festival of Speed is a well-known annual event. The noise level is monitored and categorised, so if you're after peace and quiet it's worth checking the website calendar, which shows the noise category for each day when events are taking place.

A more pleasant and peaceful option is a visit to West Dean Gardens, located just a couple of miles northwest of the car park. A place of beauty and tranquillity, there are 90 acres (36ha) of grounds and a circular arboretum walk. Combining a visit here with this memorable downland walk would make for a lovely day.

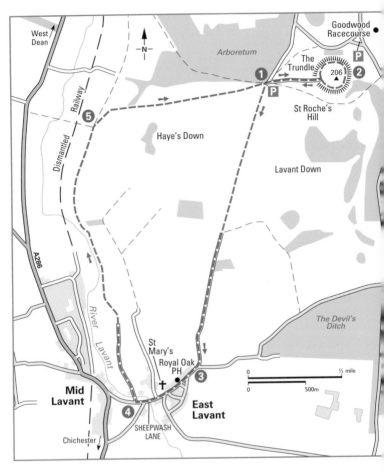

1. From the car park, make your way up the track towards the masts. Continue ahead at the top, then turn right onto the ramparts to do a complete circuit.

2. Drop down the ramparts and walk round and back down to the car park. Turn left downhill on a stony track, heading south towards Chichester and East Lavant. The views are glorious, the scene dominated by a vast patchwork of fields and hedgerows, and the distant spire of Chichester Cathedral acting as a useful directional landmark. On the way down you may also spot in the distance to the southwest Portsmouth's striking Spinnaker Tower. This track is part of a popular cycle route, so look out for cyclists who come rushing up behind you, leaving clouds of dust in their wake on a summer's day. Your walk may also be accompanied by the drone of light aircraft overhead as planes

take off and land at nearby Goodwood aerodrome. In due course, trees, bushes and margins of underbrush obscure the fine views in places.

3. After 1.5 miles (2.4km) reach the village of East Lavant, turn right, and walk along the main street. Pass the Royal Oak and the parish church and cross the bridge over the weed-choked River Lavant. Veer right just beyond it into Sheepwash Lane, and pause for a moment or two to study the simple war memorial at the corner of the road. Farmers once washed their sheep in the river here, hence the name.

4. Bear right over a brick bridge after 70yds (64m) at the sign for Staple House Farm to follow the bridleway. Pass the turning on the right that leads to the farm, and keep straight on. The track ahead can be flooded after periods of heavy rain, especially in winter. The bridleway divides into two parallel paths at one point, but your choice of route doesn't matter as they unite further on. Keep ahead, passing a left turn towards some waterworks. The path becomes enclosed by trees and scrub before the surroundings become once again open and exposed, with the walk keeping to the right-hand side of the boundary fence. Continue to a gate and 25yds (23m) beyond it arrive at a fingerpost marking a junction of bridleways, ignoring another gate on the left.

5. Veer half right at this point, following the outline of the path as it runs diagonally across the grassy slope. The path reaches a gate in the line of trees. Looking back, there are fine downland views stretching to Kingley Vale on the horizon, with the A286 threading its way across the landscape. Pass through the gate and follow the path between fields, the spire of Chichester Cathedral seen over to the right, reaching skyward. Wild poppies grow in the field-edges here, adding an extra dash of colour. A large house with sash windows and a slate roof looms into view ahead as you approach the end of the walk. Continue past the house back to the car park.

Where to eat and drink
The Royal Oak at East Lavant is more of a restaurant than a pub, with a small bar and a terrace. Children and dogs are allowed inside. You might find an ice cream van at Seven Points.

What to see
In summer, keep an eye out for flowers such as harebells, scabious and orchids and downland birds like skylarks, yellowhammers, buzzards and kestrels. The skylark epitomises the Downs, with its distinctive high-pitched melodies. Males hover and sing at a considerable height, usually appearing to the naked eye as just a dot in the sky. The Downs are famous for their butterflies, so look out, too, for chalkhill blues, marbled whites and silver-washed fritillaries.

While you're there
Have a look round East Lavant on the River Lavant, a winterbourne which is sometimes dry for years at a time. The river, which rises near East Dean, passes through Chichester to reach Chichester Harbour.

CHICHESTER'S SPIRE AND CANAL

DISTANCE/TIME	4 miles (6.4km) / 1hr 50mins
ASCENT/GRADIENT	Negligible
PATHS	Urban walkways, tow path and field paths, several stiles
LANDSCAPE	Mixture of city streets and open countryside
SUGGESTED MAP	AA Walker's Map 20 Chichester & The South Downs
START/FINISH	Grid reference: SU859044
DOG FRIENDLINESS	On lead in Chichester and farmland. Off lead by canal
PARKING	Southgate pay and display car park off Avenue de Chartres
PUBLIC TOILETS	At larger car park over the other side of the Avenue de Chartres and elsewhere in Chichester, including the cathedral

A stroll through the quaint streets of Chichester is the only way to appreciate all that this small but very beautiful cathedral city has to offer. Chichester's origins date back as far as the late Iron Age, and it was settled by the Romans in about AD 200. They built the walls, which can still be clearly identified.

During the Middle Ages, the city witnessed the building of the great cathedral and its precincts. Later, in the boom years of the 18th century, Chichester really came into its own when wealthy merchants, engaged in the shipping industry and the corn trade, began to build many of the fine houses and civic buildings you see today.

From the car park it is only a matter of minutes before you find yourself right at the heart of Chichester. Make the cathedral your first port of call. This is the focal point of the city, the Mother Church of the Diocese of Chichester. The spire, a notable local landmark, collapsed in 1861 and was rebuilt under the supervision of Sir George Gilbert Scott, who was also responsible for St Pancras station and the Albert Memorial in London. Ranging from Norman to Perpendicular in style, this magnificent building includes the site of a shrine to St Richard, Bishop of Chichester in the 13th century, tapestries by John Piper and Romanesque stone carvings. Another memorable feature is Graham Sutherland's painting, which depicts Christ appearing to St Mary Magdalen on the first Easter morning.

From the cathedral the walk heads down West Street to the intricately decorated Market Cross, built at the beginning of the 16th century and considered to be one of the finest of its kind in the country. It was Bishop Story who made a gift of the cross to the city. He also endowed the Prebendal School in West Street. Situated at the hub of the Roman street plan and distinguished by its flying buttresses, the cross was built to provide shelter for traders who came to Chichester to sell their wares. Make your way up North Street to the Council House, built in 1731 and famous for its huge stone lion and Roman stone. The Latin inscription records the dedication of a Roman temple to Neptune and Minerva. From here it's an easy stroll south to the Pallants, a compact network of narrow streets and elegant houses. Leaving the city, the walk then follows the Chichester section of the Portsmouth and Arundel Canal south to the village of Hunston. Buildings change and cities continue to evolve, but Chichester's most famous landmark, the elegant spire of its cathedral, remains in view for part of this pleasant walk out and back along the canal.

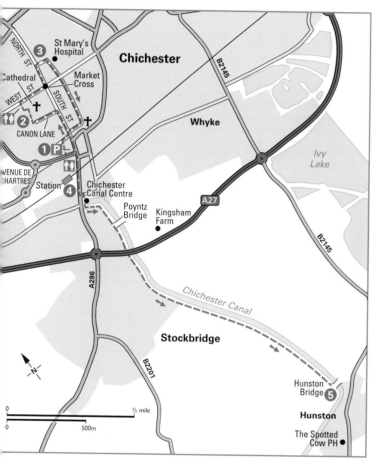

1. Leave the car park at the northeast corner (the other end from the entrance), to go under an arch between shops. Turn left into South Street by the Fountain pub. Bear left through an archway leading into Canon Lane. Turn right into St Richard's Walk and approach Chichester Cathedral.

2. Swing left at the cloisters, then left again to keep the stone wall on your left. Make for the West Door and pass the Bell Tower to reach West Street. Bear right here. Across the road is a converted church, now a pub. The north face

of Chichester Cathedral is clearly seen as you head along West Street. On reaching the Market Cross, turn left into North Street and bear right immediately beyond the historic many-arched, red-brick Council House into Lion Street.

3. Walk along to St Martin's Square and opposite you at this point is St Mary's Hospital. Turn right and pass the Hole in the Wall pub to reach East Street. Glance to the left and you can pick out the Corn Exchange. Go straight over into North Pallant and walk along to Pallant House Gallery, one of England's finest collections of modern art. Head straight on into South Pallant and follow the road round to the right as it becomes Old Market Avenue, passing Christ Church on the left. Turn left at the next junction and keep ahead at the following junction into Southgate.

4. Cross the railway at Chichester station and then swing left to reach the canal basin. Follow the tow path around the right side of the basin to Poyntz Bridge, dated 1820, and continue to the next bridge, which carries the A27 Chichester bypass. Keep going as far as the next footbridge, Hunston Bridge (confusingly labelled Poyntz Bridge on Ordnance Survey maps, since this is where the latter was originally situated before being relocated).

5. Admire the view from the bridge of the canal with the cathedral in the distance, the scene depicted in a painting by J M W Turner. Retrace your steps towards Chichester. Just after crossing the railway line, turn left then right to return to the car park.

Where to eat and drink

There are dozens of restaurants, cafés and pubs in Chichester, including the Cloisters Café at the cathedral and the acclaimed restaurant at the Pallant House Gallery. The former uses fair-trade suppliers; the latter uses home-grown and locally sourced produce for its seasonal menus. There's also The Spotted Cow at Hunston.

What to see

In addition to the remains of the Roman city walls, there is St Mary's Hospital of the Blessed Virgin Mary in St Martin's Square, founded between 1158 and 1170. Originally a hospital, it later became almshouses. In the nearby Pallants is Queen Anne-style Pallant House, built by Chichester wine merchant Henry Peckham in 1712.

While you're there

Enjoy a trip on the tree-lined Chichester Canal. It's part of the Portsmouth and Arundel Canal, built to link with other rivers and navigations to form an inland waterway between London and Portsmouth. Trips can be booked at the Chichester Canal Centre at the canal basin. Designed by John Rennie and opened in 1822, the canal acted as a through route until 1855 and the Chichester stretch was built to take ships.

SHULBREDE PRIORY AND COMMONS

DISTANCE/TIME	2.75 miles (4.4km) / 1hr 30min
ASCENT/GRADIENT	252ft (77m) / ▲ ▲
PATHS	Woodland paths and tracks, field paths and tracks, some lanes
LANDSCAPE	Intimate and deep winding valleys, coppiced woodland and heathland
SUGGESTED MAP	AA Walker's Map 23 Guildford, Farnham & The Downs
START/FINISH	Grid reference: SU864315
DOG FRIENDLINESS	On lead through Newland Cottage's horse paddocks and along lanes. On Lynchmere Common there could be a few Shetland cattle grazing
PARKING	Along the lane through Lynchmere Common either side of the Lynchmere Society information board
PUBLIC TOILETS	None on route

Lynchmere and the Golden Valley, through which this walk passes, have some gorgeous scenery. At the northern border of Sussex, the area feels more like parts of Surrey in its intimate, heavily wooded and secluded nature. The walk passes through areas of coppiced sweet chestnut and across an attractive common that is being actively managed by the Lynchmere Society through scrub and bracken clearance, cattle grazing and hazel coppicing.

Sussex seems unusually rich in the remnants of small abbeys and priories, and Lynchmere has a fine example. From the road, Shulbrede Priory looks like a fairly normal 16th- or 17th-century stone house, but it is in fact part of the medieval prior's lodging and of the canon's refectory or dining hall, and mainly dates to the 13th century. Within the courtyard formerly the cloisters is an elegant arcade with trefoil arches that was part of the lavatorium, the canon's washhouse.

Founded as an Augustinian priory in about 1190 by Ralph de Arderne and originally named Woolynchmere Priory, it had an aisled church of some scale, being 140ft (43m) long with a central crossing tower. The priory sits within a moat, which can be seen from the road. When the priory was converted to an Elizabethan house, a medieval partition inserted in the hall above the undercroft was painted with figures of birds and animals depicting the Nativity, with ladies in Tudor costume and even a building that probably represents the priory. In the 17th century the arms of James I were added.

From the outside, St Peter's Church at Lynchmere looks a church typical of these sandstone hills. However, a little 13th-century belfry tower was added to a Norman nave, and when you go inside you see the round-headed Norman west doorway arch, now leading into a vestry. Next to this are the supports for the east wall of the tower, an arcade of three mid-13th-century arches carried on very tall slender columns. It is as if the belfry, of the dimensions of the more usual timber one, has been petrified and the supporting posts also transformed into stone. This unexpected sight gives the little church a surprisingly monumental interior.

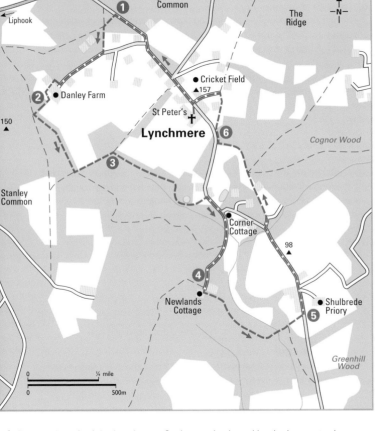

1. Pass to the left of the Lynchmere Society notice board by the lane onto the footpath across the wooded common. Immediately go through a kissing gate, follow the Serpent's Trail symbol to bear half left across the wooded common to another kissing gate ('end of access land' sign), and follow a path between fences. At the end bear right along a lane, leaving it at a cattle grid to continue ahead down the grassy slope to skirt to the right of Danley Farm.

2. Cross a driveway and go forward along the field-edge to a kissing gate on the edge of the wood. Through this follow the footpath posts left, then right, climbing, and bear left at a four-way junction to walk within the edge of the

woods, beside a valley with Danley Farm at its head. The path then enters the woods, mostly oak ,ash, ilex and sweet chestnut coppicing. Shortly the path bears left through a bridle gate and you continue ahead to the valley floor.

3. At a footpath post ignore a gate into a field and bear right, still within the woodland edge. Where the field away to the left ends, turn right downhill, then left at a signpost and soon past a pond on your left, and cross a footbridge to continue ahead past a field to reach a lane. Bear right along the lane and where the lane bears left continue ahead, to the right of Corner Cottage. Continue ahead on a track, at first on the edge of woods, then within.

4. At paddocks go left through a gate at the end of the first paddock and before reaching Newlands Cottage. Almost immediately go over a wooden 'Baldwin Bridge' and through two gates, then down the inside edge of woodland. The path turns rights at the bottom, through the fir plantation. At a path junction bear left and at the crest keep left at the next signpost.

5. Turn left along a lane and pass the entrance to Shulbrede Priory on your right. Continue uphill, then down to a bridge. Cross the bridge and almost immediately bear half right on an unmarked footpath into the woods. At a drive cross over and continue up a woodland track, soon passing to the left of a garage. Now on a path within woods climb to the crest and continue, a silver birch copse on your right. At a footpath junction bear left and climb towards the road.

6. Just before the road go right and climb steeply. Levelling out, go left at a junction where a field appears ahead, then left again through a gate, and skirt a cricket ground. Continue to the road and bear left to visit Lynchmere church. Then retrace your steps and continue ahead to end the walk at the common.

Where to eat and drink

Liphook, over the border in Hampshire, has a few pubs and L&S Gift & Coffee House in The Square. If you prefer a more rural location, the nearest pub to Lynchmere is the Prince of Wales in Hammervale, also over the Hampshire border. This offers good food and cask ales.

What to see

As you walk on Lynchmere Common you may see the Shetland cattle grazing. Introduced to help restore the common's wood pasture, these small, hardy cattle are thought to have evolved from cattle brought to the Shetland Islands by the Vikings. Either black and white or a deep russet red, they live happily on rough grazing and once also grazed Ebernoe Common.

While you're there

A mile (1.6km) or so west of Lynchmere, on the Liphook to Midhurst road, is Hollycombe Steam in the Country (open summer Sundays and bank holidays and most of August). It has everything from standard-gauge, narrow-gauge and miniature steam railways, traction engines and beam engines to steam fairground rides.

VIEWS AT KINGLEY VALE

DISTANCE/TIME	5 miles (8km) / 2hrs
ASCENT/GRADIENT	440ft (134m) / ▲ ▲
PATHS	Mostly woodland paths and downland tracks
LANDSCAPE	Dense woodland and rolling downland
SUGGESTED MAP	AA Walker's Map 20 Chichester & The South Downs
START/FINISH	Grid reference: SU815126
DOG FRIENDLINESS	Under control in Stoughton village. Elsewhere off lead unless signs state otherwise
PARKING	Free car park at Stoughton Down
PUBLIC TOILETS	None on route

You might not expect to find the largest yew forest in Europe tucked away in the South Downs, but that's exactly where it is. This remote downland landscape, covering more than 200 acres (81ha) is cloaked with 30,000 yew trees. Once a wartime artillery range, Kingley Vale became one of Britain's first nature reserves in 1952. Today, it is managed by Natural England.

Silent, isolated and thankfully inaccessible by car, the grove of ancient yew trees at Kingley Vale is a haven for ramblers and naturalists. The walk skirts the forest, but if you have the time to explore, the effort is certainly worthwhile. The yew is one of the UK's finest trees and can live up to 2,000 years. It is usually a large but squat tree, its branches and dark green needles conspiring to create a dense evergreen canopy which allows little light to filter through to the forest floor. With their deep red trunks, branches and shallow roots twisted into monstrous shapes and gargoyle faces, some of the yews at Kingley Vale are thought to be over 500 years old.

Even on the sunniest summer's day, the scene amid the tangle of boughs is eerily dark, strange and mystical, like something from the pages of a children's fairy tale. The yew has always featured strongly in folklore and, according to legend, this place was a meeting point for witches who engaged in pagan rites and wove magic spells here. Danes and druids are also believed to haunt the vale.

Various theories about the origin of the forest have been suggested, but it is thought that the site marks the spot where a 9th-century battle against the Vikings took place. Some sources suggest the trees were planted here to guide pilgrims travelling across the South Downs to Canterbury. Long before the yews began to grow, Bronze Age kings were buried here, confirmed by various tumuli on the Ordnance Survey map.

The trees may be the dominant feature at Kingley Vale but the grove is teeming with wildlife. The delightful green woodpecker, noted for its distinctive colouring, inhabits the reserve, one of 57 species of breeding bird found here. The bee orchid blooms in June, while mountain sheep and wild fallow deer keep the turf short for 200 other species of flower. If you're lucky, you might spot a fox or a kestrel.

Beginning just outside the village of Stoughton, the walk immediately makes for dense woodland before climbing quite steeply to the spectacular viewpoint overlooking Kingley Vale. The reserve, renowned for its ecological importance, covers the southern chalk slopes of 655ft (206m) high Bow Hill, and from this high ground the views are tremendous.

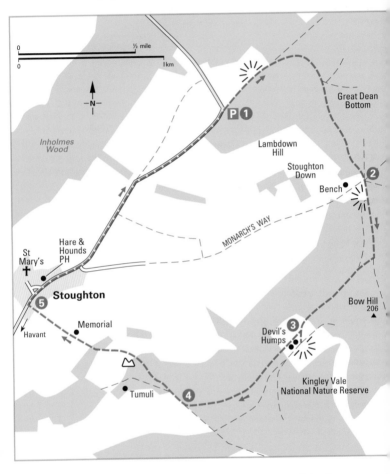

1. Take the bridleway (signposted from the car park entrance), leading away from the road and through a metal barrier, skirting dense woodland. There are striking views on the left over well-wooded countryside. Keep right at a fork and follow the stony path as it curves to the right. Veer slightly right as signposted at the next waymarked fork, and begin a gradual ascent beneath the boughs of beech and oak trees.

2. Eventually break cover from the trees at a major junction of waymarked tracks. Go straight on, looking to the right for spectacular views. After 125yds (41m), fork left at the next bridleway sign and join a path running parallel to the track. Cut between trees and keep going for 0.25 miles (400m) until you

reach a waymarker post. Fork right here. Keep to the waymarked path as it runs down the slope. Rejoin the stony track, turning left to follow it up the slope towards Bow Hill.

3. About 30 yards (27m) after the Devil's Humps, veer left off the path by a sign for Kingley Vale Nature Reserve to enjoy the magnificent vistas across the downland countryside. The view to the north, over remote woodland and downland, is impressive enough, but the panorama to the south is particularly outstanding. Immediately below you are the trees of Kingley Vale. Return to the path near the nature reserve sign, and continue the previous direction along the route, keeping to the right of the Devil's Hump and re-entering the forest.

4. Bear right at the next main junction and follow the bridle track alongside a field. On the left are glimpses of Chichester Harbour, with its complex network of watery channels and sprawling mudflats, and the Isle of Wight beyond. Soon enter the trees and ignore a left fork; near here are more ancient burial tumuli. Follow the track down through the woodland and out into the open, Stoughton in view below. Pass a memorial to a young Polish airman whose Hurricane crashed near here after a dog-fight during World War II. Turn right at the road.

5. Pass the entrance to St Mary's Church on the left, followed by the Hare & Hounds pub. Continue through the village and on the right is the Monarch's Way. Follow the road out of Stoughton back to the car park.

Where to eat and drink

Have a picnic by the Devil's Humps or stop off towards the end of the walk at the Hare & Hounds in Stoughton. This striking flint building dates back to around the 17th century and was originally built as two cottages. Choose from a good snack menu, which includes sandwiches and baguettes, or go for something more exciting such as roast beef salad, ribs or steak. Everything is cooked on the premises and there are various game dishes in season. There is a terrace in front, and children and dogs are welcome.

While you're there

Visit Stoughton's 11th-century cruciform church of St Mary. The exterior is barn-like, bulky even, and inside it is unexpectedly spacious. The south transept was converted into a tower in the 14th century, the nave is over 30ft (9m) high and there is a striking Norman arch with a triple layer of roll mouldings.

A HARBOUR WALK
AT WEST ITCHENOR

DISTANCE/TIME	3.5 miles (5.7km) / 1hr 30min
ASCENT/GRADIENT	Negligible
PATHS	Shoreline, field tracks and paths, several stiles
LANDSCAPE	Open farmland and coastal scenery
SUGGESTED MAP	AA Walker's Map 20 Chichester & The South Downs
START/FINISH	Grid reference: SU798012
DOG FRIENDLINESS	Waterside paths are ideal for dogs, but keep under control on stretches of open farmland and the short section of road. Dogs permitted on harbour water tour
PARKING	Large pay-and-display car park in West Itchenor
PUBLIC TOILETS	West Itchenor

Weekend sailors flock to Chichester's vast natural harbour, making it one of the most popular attractions on the south coast. The harbour has about 50 miles (81km) of shoreline and 17 miles (28km) of navigable channel, though there is almost no commercial traffic.

The Romans cast an approving eye over this impressive stretch of water and established a military base and harbour at nearby Fishbourne after the Claudian invasion of Britain in AD 43. Charles II had a fondness for the area too and kept a yacht here.

Situated at the confluence of the Bosham and Chichester channels of the estuary is the sailing village of Itchenor, with its main street of picturesque houses and cottages running down to the waterfront. Originally named Icenor, this small settlement started life as a remote, sparsely populated community, but by the 18th century it had begun to play a vital role in the shipbuilding industry. Small warships were built here by the merchants of Chichester, though in later years shipbuilding ceased altogether, and any trace of its previous prosperity disappeared beneath the houses and the harbour mud. However, the modern age of leisure and recreation has seen a revival in boat building and yachting, and today Itchenor is once again bustling with boat yards, sailors and chandlers.

However, there is much more to Chichester Harbour than sailing. Take a stroll along the harbour edge and you will find there is much to capture the attention. With its intertidal habitats, the harbour is a haven for plant life and wildlife. Wading birds such as the curlew, redshank and dunlin can be seen using their differently shaped bills to extract food from the ecologically rich mudflats, and terns may be spotted plunging to catch fish. Plants include sea lavender and glasswort, and many of them are able to resist flooding and changing saltiness. Salt marsh is one of the typical habitats of Chichester Harbour, and the plants which make up the marsh grow in different places according to how often they are flooded. Stand at West Itchenor and you can look across the water towards neighbouring Bosham, pronounced 'Bozzum'. Better still, take the ferry over there and explore the delights of this harbour village. It was from here that Harold left for Normandy before the Norman Conquest of 1066. 'The sea creek, the green field, the grey church,' wrote Tennyson and this sums up perfectly the charm of this unspoilt corner of Sussex. Take a little time to look at the Church of the Holy Trinity and its Saxon tower base while you're there.

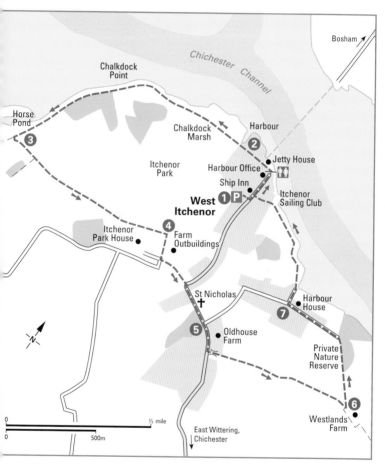

1. From the car park walk along to the road and bear left, heading towards the harbour front. Pass the Ship Inn and go to the water's edge. Look for the harbour office and the toilets, and follow the footpath to the left of Jetty House.

2. Cut between hedging and fencing to reach a boat yard and then continue ahead on the clear surfaced path, passing a permissive path on the left that leads back to the car park. Keep left at a fork and shortly the path breaks cover to run by the harbour and its expanses of mudflats. Cross Chalkdock Marsh and continue on the waterside path.

3. Keep going until you reach a footpath sign with a marker for the New Lipchis Way. Turn left here by a sturdy old oak tree and pass through a pinch-gate to follow the path away from the harbour edge, keeping to the right-hand boundary of the field. Cross another pinch-gate to join a track on a bend and continue ahead, still maintaining the same direction. Pass Itchenor Park House on the right and approach some farm outbuildings.

4. Turn right by a brick-and-flint farm outbuilding and follow the path, soon merging with a concrete track. Walk ahead to reach the next junction and turn left by a white gate, down to the road. Keep ahead here and soon you reach the little 13th-century church of St Nicholas, with Itchenor Village Pond just beyond.

5. Follow the road beyond Oldhouse Farm and then turn left at the footpath sign to cross a footbridge. Keep to the right of a barn and follow the path straight ahead across the field. Pass a line of trees and keep alongside a ditch on the right into the next field. The path follows the hedge line, making for the field corner. Ahead are the buildings of Westlands Farm.

6. Turn sharp left by the footpath sign and follow the path across the field. Skirt the woodland, part of a private nature reserve, and veer left at the entrance to the Spinney. Follow the residential drive to Harbour House.

7. Turn right just beyond it and follow the path along the edge of the harbour. Keep going along here until you reach Itchenor Sailing Club. Bear left and walk up the drive to the road. Opposite you should be the Ship Inn. Turn left to return to the car park.

Where to eat and drink
The Ship Inn at West Itchenor dates back to 1803 and was largely rebuilt after a fire in the 1930s. The spacious interior fills up on summer weekends, but there is a good choice of food.

What to see
Just over halfway round the walk is the 13th-century Church of St Nicholas, dedicated to the patron saint of children and seafarers. The little church, which has a lych gate, is usually open and inside there are some fascinating treasures. There have been a number of alterations and additions over the years.

While you're there
Enjoy a water tour of Chichester Harbour during the summer months, or go in winter when there are regular trips for birding, accompanied by an expert guide. These tours enable you to appreciate the harbour's treasures first-hand and see at close quarters some of the many vessels that use it. There are about 12,000 resident boats, with many visiting yachts from the USA, the Far East and Europe.

WIDE HORIZONS AT WEST WITTERING

DISTANCE/TIME	5 miles (8km) / 2hr 30min
ASCENT/GRADIENT	Negligible
PATHS	Beach and water-side paths, road and private drives
LANDSCAPE	Wide views, natural tidal inlet
SUGGESTED MAP	AA Walker's Map 20 Chichester & The South Downs
START/FINISH	Grid reference: SZ772978
DOG FRIENDLINESS	Off lead on harbour-side paths. On lead in West Wittering. Dogs excluded from main swimming beach from May to September. Keep under control on East Head
PARKING	Large fee-paying car park at West Wittering beach
PUBLIC TOILETS	West Wittering beach and village

The seaside community of West Wittering is a genteel place, tucked away from the rest of Sussex on a peninsula at the mouth of Chichester Harbour. Despite the hordes of summer visitors who flock to the beach, it retains a dignified air, evoking distant memories of how small seaside towns used to be. The village evolved mainly during the first half of the 20th century, though some elderly residents recall this stretch of coast before it became fashionable, when open fields extended to the superb beach, providing a natural playground for children.

East Head, the slender spit of sand and shingle dunes at the mouth of Chichester Harbour, has changed dramatically during the last two centuries, influenced by the elements. In 1786 the spit pointed across the entrance of the harbour towards Hayling Island, but since then its position has moved and it now points north. In November 1963 part of East Head was breached by high spring tides and its future looked uncertain. The following year the dunes were artificially reshaped and stabilised before being handed to the National Trust in 1966. Work to restore this sensitive natural feature of the Sussex coast has continued ever since. Visitors are requested to use the boardwalks to avoid trampling the marram grass, which is essential for helping stabilise the sand, and to stay out of the fenced- or roped-off areas.

The walk is most enjoyable at low tide when large expanses of sand are revealed. Between East Head and the mainland is an area of salt marsh known as Snowhill Creek, which provides a feeding ground for thousands of birds. Among the large numbers of wintering waders and wildfowl found here are Brent geese, shelduck, redshank and curlew. Up to 45,000 Brent geese fly into Chichester Harbour from September to December. Of that number around 5,000 settle at Snowhill Creek and graze the fields of West Wittering Estate.

Out on the shingle banks of East Head, ringed plovers nest. Their eggs are camouflaged to look like pebbles. Common and grey seals are both found in Chichester Harbour. When the tide is out you may spot them on mud banks.

The West Wittering Estate company was formed in 1952 by local residents who clubbed together to buy the land to prevent it from being developed as a holiday complex and to preserve it for public enjoyment. This is a good walk at any time of the year, though best avoided on sunny summer weekends when the beach can be very crowded.

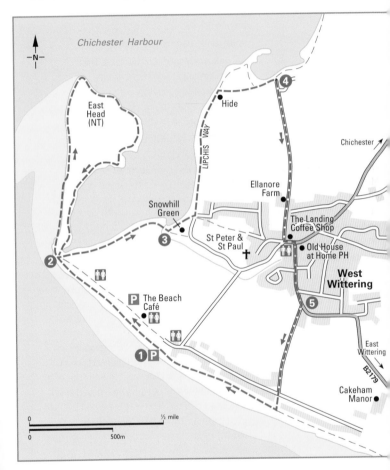

1. Follow the drive through the extensive car park, and join the parallel shore path at the earliest opportunity. Pass a row of charming beach huts and a toilet block on the right. Continue ahead towards the mouth of Chichester Harbour, with Hayling Island seen on the far side. Bearing to the right with the beach, head sharper right for the East Head National Trust sign at the foot of a dune.

2. Follow the beach round the sand dune spit (if you do go onto the dunes, use the boardwalks). After completing the circuit, bear left along the path beside

Chichester Harbour and look to the right for a glimpse of the tower at Cakeham Manor. A new flood defence has been built along here, the path running along the top of the embankment. Continue to the grassy open space of Snowhill Green, keeping along the left-hand side. Snow Hill, the part of West Wittering between the church and Chichester Harbour, has been suggested as the original Roman landing site in Britain.

3. Pass a footpath on the right and carry on along the harbour edge. Leaving West Wittering behind, the scrub-bordered path heads northwards, with open farmland on the right and the harbour and marsh landscape on the left. Eventually it bends right by a bird hide and seat. Continue along the tree-shaded footpath.

4. Turn right at the next footpath sign by a gate. Walk along Ellanore Lane, passing Ellanore Farm. On reaching the road, opposite the public conveniences, turn right if you want to visit the church. To continue on the main route, turn left to reach a junction and then bear right to walk through West Wittering. Pass the Old House at Home pub, and further along the road continue past Seaward Drive on the left, a private estate.

5. As the road bends left, cross to the right and take Berry Barn Lane, along which runs a bridleway. Follow the lane, and again the tower at Cakeham Manor can be seen just across the fields. On reaching the signs for East Strand and West Strand, go straight on to follow a path between panel fencing and bushes. With the beach ahead, turn right towards East Head and follow the path over the greensward. On the right is a row of striking villas, many of them discreetly screened by trees and hedges. The path continues over sand dunes. Beyond the villas, swing right through one of several gaps along the hedge to return to the car park.

Where to eat and drink

The Beach Café at West Wittering beach has a coffee shop and take-away, and there are also several outlets selling ice cream and drinks. In the village try The Landing coffee shop, which serves coffee and cakes as well as light lunches. Nearby is the Old House at Home, which offers a varied home-made menu that changes regularly.

What to see

Cakeham Manor, originally a grand palace belonging to the Bishops of Chichester, lies close to the route of the walk. Its most prominent feature is the tower which was added to the house in the 16th century. Neither the house nor the tower is open to the public.

While you're there

Visit the church of St Peter and St Paul in West Wittering. Dating to the 12th century, it's a lovely peaceful place to call in at, especially after a windswept walk. It is, in fact, the third or fourth church on this site, the earliest built around AD 770, shortly after St Wilfrid started converting the South Saxons (from whom Sussex takes its name) to Christianity.

TITLES IN THE SERIES

- 50 Walks in Berkshire & Buckinghamshire
- 50 Walks in the Brecon Beacons & South Wales
- 50 Walks in Cornwall
- 50 Walks in the Cotswolds
- 50 Walks in Derbyshire
- 50 Walks in Devon
- 50 Walks in Dorset
- 50 Walks in Durham & Northumberland
- 50 Walks in Essex
- 50 Walks in Gloucestershire
- 50 Walks in Hampshire & the Isle of Wight
- 50 Walks in Herefordshire & Worcestershire
- 50 Walks in Hertfordshire
- 50 Walks in Kent
- 50 Walks in the Lake District
- 50 Walks in London
- 50 Walks in Norfolk
- 50 Walks in North Yorkshire
- 50 Walks in Oxfordshire
- 50 Walks in the Peak District
- 50 Walks in Shropshire
- 50 Walks in Snowdonia & North Wales
- 50 Walks in Somerset
- 50 Walks in Staffordshire
- 50 Walks in Suffolk
- 50 Walks in Surrey
- 50 Walks in Sussex & the South Downs
- 50 Walks in Warwickshire & West Midlands
- 50 Walks in West Yorkshire
- 50 Walks in Wiltshire
- 50 Walks in the Yorkshire Dales